The Rationalization of Russia

The

Rationalization

of Russia

by George Bernard Shaw

Edited with an Introduction
by Harry M. Geduld

INDIANA UNIVERSITY PRESS

BLOOMINGTON

CONTENTS

Editor's Introduction

Bernard Shaw in Russia

Among the recently acquired manuscripts in the British Museum Shaw collection is Additional 50677, a typescript with holograph corrections, entitled "The Rationalization of Russia." The work, which is unfinished, consists of a preface and one chapter, written in South Africa during 1932, the year following GBS's only visit to Russia.

The unfinished book was an indirect outcome of Shaw's unexpectedly protracted vacation in South Africa. While seated at the wheel of an unfamiliar car, he mistook the accelerator for the clutch, and he and his wife, Charlotte, were hurled into a ditch. GBS was merely bruised, but Charlotte, who was rather seriously injured, was confined to her bed for five weeks. Shaw occupied the time by writing *The Black Girl in Search of God* and "The Rationalization of Russia." But the manuscript on Russia was evidently abandoned even before the Shaws returned to England.

However, while it was still a work-in-progress, sections of "The Rationalization of Russia" were dispatched to England to be typed by Shaw's secretary, Blanche Patch. The text that follows is based on the typescript copy and incorporates holograph corrections that were undertaken by Shaw after his return from South Africa.

Shaw's abandonment of the manuscript will seem curious only to readers who are unfamiliar with his Prefaces of the 'thirties. *On the Rocks, Too True to be Good,* and *The Simpleton of the Unexpected Isles* resound with memorable echoes of "The Rationalization of Russia." Indeed, there is an ideological continuity between the unfinished manuscript and the political prefaces which suggests that material that would have contributed toward the completion of the one was diverted and poured into the others. Thus in many respects "The Rationalization of Russia" may be considered a sketch-plan for the last phase of Shaw's political writings. It contains a brilliant satirical exposition of the history of modern Europeon capitalism and its apparent debacle in the 1930s, and a scathing critique of international banking and stock exchange transactions. Shaw's target is the corruption of predatory Western society, and his remedy is the replacement of modern capitalist predacity by a political system of enforced honesty. He writes as a revolutionist fired by the achievements of the U.S.S.R. during the first flush of the Stalinist era and the Five-Year Plan. In some of his wittiest and most sparkling prose he explains the spectrum of European socialist parties and the seesaw policies of British Laborites under Ramsay MacDonald. He provides an inimitable Shavian history of nineteenth- and twentieth-century revolutionists in Russia, and caps his apologia for the Soviet social and punitive system with a paradoxical critique of Marxism.

"The Rationalization of Russia" provides eloquent testimony to the argument in *Man and Superman* that effectiveness of assertion is the alpha and omega of style. "He who has nothing to assert will go as far in power of style as its momentousness and his conviction will carry him. Disprove his assertion after it is made, yet its style remains." It is unthinkable that Shavian prose of such brilliance and vitality should remain in the obscurity of an unpublished manuscript.

Readers who are already aware of Shaw's long flirtation with Soviet Communism are unlikely to be surprised by the political content of the fragment. Those who question whether GBS really meant what he said or who conclude that the entire piece is a deliberate "leg-pull" will be unable to see the fragment in its true perspective. The essential query is not whether Shaw said what he meant but whether he ever said anything he did not mean. In *The Intelligent Woman's Guide* he remarked that "the people who exasperate me most are those who have really read the book, or think they have. I took the utmost pains to make it intelligible, clear, lucid, unambiguous, simple and unmistakeable. The result appears to be that only one man in the civilized world has understood it, and that man is Albert Einstein. I begin to think that lucidity is self-defeating. . . . People cannot take it in until they have reintroduced all the adulterations from their own home supplies. Then they expatiate, at my expense, on their own adulterations."

Toward the end of his life, in *Sixteen Self Sketches*, Shaw published a statement to the effect that he had been a coward until Marx made a man of him and gave him a faith. GBS was a Marxist fourteen years before Lenin discovered *Das Kapital,* and he was preaching socialism and communism long before the October Revolution. Later he became an admirer of Stalin just as he had been a eulogist of Lenin. When Trotsky split with Lenin over the issue of world revolution versus socialism in one country, Shaw approved Stalin's line, in which he discerned a variation on the Fabian policy of the inevitability of gradualness. Hesketh Pearson has described how, after 1917, "the Bolshevists were, if possible, more venomously execrated by the British socialists and labour leaders than by the capitalist parties. This lasted until, at a public meeting of the Fabian Society, Shaw rose and said, 'We are socialists. The Russian side is our side.'" It remained Shaw's side until the day of his death.

The immediate background of "The Rationalization of Russia" is Shaw's brief visit to the Soviet Union, an experience that confirmed his high opinions of the new regime. He had avoided making the trip until 1931 because he was convinced that the Soviet system would not be seen at its best during the first flush of N.E.P. reactions to the excesses of war Communism.

Unlike his wife, Shaw hated traveling, and it is possible that he would never have visited Russia at all if the Marquis of Lothian had not prevailed upon him to make the journey.

He set off from Victoria Station, London, on July 18, 1931. On the platform, surrounded by a group of apprehensive friends and by the usual mob of reporters, he smilingly declared how much he was looking forward to his Russian trip. The Fabian Society had been promised an account of his impressions of Russia, and there was every expectation of a Shavian sequel to H. G. Wells's *Russia in the Shadows*.

Unfortunately Shaw did not complete the later sections of "The Rationalization of Russia," in which, presumably, he would have dealt at length with his visit to the Soviet Union. It also appears that he did not keep a travel diary of his experiences in Russia. The following account of his tour has, therefore, been reconstructed from a variety of sources, primarily from press reports in British, American, and Soviet newspapers. In particular, specific statements by Shaw are quoted from *The New York Times,* the London *Times, Observer,* and *Daily Worker.* Factual details on the Krynin episode were taken from Eugene Lyons' *Assignment in Utopia.*

During his travels GBS was usually accompanied by Charlotte, but on this occasion she decided to remain at home. Shaw was to visit the Soviet Union in the company of some highly critical personal friends who were unashamedly capitalist, and whose affection for GBS did not in any way influence their abhorrence of his political views. First and foremost there was "Nancy," Lady Astor, the Tsarina of Cliveden, who had promised Charlotte that she would look after "Joey" and see that he kept his beard clean. Palely loitering in her shadow were Viscount Astor and the Astors' son, David. The presence of the Marquis of Lothian (Phillip Kerr), an eminent Liberal and former secretary to Lloyd George, gave even more substance to the prevailing impression that a blue-blooded elite was accompanying an aristocrat of the intellect. The plebeians who made up the rest of the party included J. W. Mallin, head of London's Toynbee Hall Social Welfare Center, Gertrude Ely of Philadelphia, and Sidney D. Gamble, a sociologist from Cincinnati, Ohio.

The U.S.S.R. had been alerted on July 9, when the party applied for their visas. Shortly afterward Moscow received a statement from Shaw in the form of a telegram to Bella Illes, General Secretary of the International Union of Revolutionary Writers. He announced that he was going to visit the Soviet Union with some friends. It would be a short visit because he had previously accepted an invitation to address the Independent Labor Summer School in Welwyn during August. He particularly requested that he should not be burdened with parades, receptions or banquets; he was coming for "serious business."

H. G. Wells had claimed that the harsh and terrible realities of the situation in Russia could not be camouflaged. His visit, in 1920, was not heralded by widespread press publicity. "In the case of special delegations," he had written, "perhaps a certain distracting tumult of receptions, bands, and speeches may be possible, and may be attempted. But it is hardly possible to dress up . . . large cities for the benefit of . . . stray visitors, wandering observantly often in different directions. Naturally, when one demands to see a school or a prison one is not shown the worst. Any country would in the circumstances show the best it had. . . ."

By contrast, Shaw's telegram was given considerable advance publicity in Russia. His special request was ignored by the Soviet authorities. Guides were briefed, receptions were organized, and a spectacular itinerary was prepared. It was, if all went according to plan, to be the perfect conducted tour. That would take care of Shaw's impressions of Russia; but what about Russia's impressions of Shaw? The Irish dramatist had an unpredictable habit of publicly expressing heretical political opinions. He was avowedly a socialist, but he had no scruples about criticizing socialism, and he had recently indulged in lavish praise of Mussolini and Italian Fascism. In his younger days Shaw had even committed the blasphemy of finding a "flaw" in Marx's theory of surplus value. He was, moreover, very wealthy and lived like a bourgeois. A friend of reactionaries and capitalists, he traveled in the company of British aristocrats and rich Americans.

Lunacharsky prepared an explanatory statement for *Izvestia* on "Bernard Shaw, Our Guest": "We realize that

Bernard Shaw is our ally. Yet we know quite well that he may sometimes execute some amazing zigzag . . . indulging in witticism at our expense . . . and do so in a manner calculated to evoke a satisfied grunt from the bourgeoisie. . . . The penetrating eye of the 'free man' will surely discern the real truth which, after all, is the only cause that the great Irish writer is always anxious to serve."

The party arrived in Berlin on July 19, Shaw quickly extricated himself from another mob of reporters and sought temporary sanctuary in the British Embassy, where he spent a peaceful Sunday afternoon. Toward evening he rejoined the Astors on the Warsaw-Moscow night express. Many reporters followed him to the station, and before the train moved off he rewarded their persistence by answering a few questions. He revealed that he had just completed a new play. His visit to Russia was temporary, but he refused to state how long he intended to stay there. In addition, he made no secret of the fact that he was tired of being plagued by swarms of reporters. One of the newspaper fraternity assured him that he would be greeted by at least five thousand reporters if he ever visited New York. "That," replied GBS, "is exactly why I don't intend to go to New York."

Three years before, *The Apple Cart* had received its world *première* in Warsaw. Shaw's plays were established favorites in the Polish theatrical repertoire, but GBS's enthusiasm for the U.S.S.R. was incomprehensible to the Poles. A few Polish newspapers noticed that Shaw had passed through Warsaw; some printed photographs of him; but his interviews with Polish reporters were apparently considered too provocative to publish.

Crossing the Polish border, the Warsaw-Moscow night express came to a halt at the little Russian town of Nigoreloye. Evidently Shaw's telegram was being honored, for there were no official welcoming delegations, no flags, no parades, no speeches, and only one journalist. As the party stepped off the train they were greeted by a small unofficial deputation: a guide who had been assigned the task of arranging the party's itinerary; Kogan, a literary critic; Ionov, a publisher; Gladkov, a writer; and Anna Louise Strong, a reporter for the *Moscow News,* an English-language newspaper printed in the U.S.S.R. The party proceeded through the new customs house, where they were shown decorative murals of Dnieprostroi.

Meanwhile, a special sleeping-car was coupled to the express. When the party emerged from the customs house Shaw looked into the sleeping-car and asked whether it had been the private carriage of the late Tsar. "It is much bigger than anything we had in Germany."

With half an hour to kill before the train refueled and moved off, most of the party climbed into the sleeping-car and settled down for the last lap of the journey to Moscow. GBS was restless. He strolled about the platform and then decided to look into the restaurant. Here the guide formally introduced him to two waitresses who were longing to meet the great Bernard Shaw. By an extraordinary coincidence they were intimately acquainted with his works. GBS was sufficiently moved by this remarkable evidence of Russian literacy to express the opinion that waitresses in England were not so well-read as their Soviet sisters.

Outside the station Nancy Astor pointed out a group of young peasant women who were engaged in heavy railroad construction work. "There," she commented. "Just as I feared. The machines are dislodging them from the farms. They have no work at home." A Russian bystander corrected her. These women were doing temporary railroad work during the slack season between sowing and reaping.

They would soon be returning to their collective farm. "Tell them to be sure and keep the men in their place," retorted Lady Astor.

Shaw was impressed by the restfulness of his reception at Nigoreloye. In Berlin the reporters had "practically mobbed" him, but here the Russians appeared to have more respect for his privacy. He was overconfident, however, for a great crowd was awaiting him in Moscow. When the train pulled into the White Russia station next morning thousands of Muscovites had turned out to greet GBS. There were loud shouts of "Hail Shaw!" Welcoming banners waved aloft and a brass band struck up in accompaniment of the official guard of honor. Shaw smiled and waved his hat to the crowd. There were even more reporters here than in Berlin: American and British contingents as well as representatives of the leading Soviet press agencies. The official reception committee was headed by bearded and leather-jacketed Khalatov, manager of Gosizdat (the State Publishing House). Lunacharsky and Karl Radek were also there. Khalatov formally welcomed the party to Moscow; then he introduced a young Englishman who had lived in Moscow for two years and intended to remain in Russia. "Good!" said Shaw. "If I was as young as you I think I should like to stay here too."

Now a way was cleared to the station exit. Two Red Army men were detached from the guard of honor and Shaw strode between them along the platform. Outside the station he was lustily applauded by a large group of "workers' correspondents." He posed briefly for motion picture cameramen and was then driven off to the Metropole hotel. There were reporters here too. They were eager to find out his first impressions of the Soviet Union; but Shaw was noncommittal. "Not yet," he said. "In a week maybe I'll tell

you something if I can't avoid it; but nothing now." Lady
Astor followed him into the elevator. Their fellow passen-
gers were a hotel servant girl and a Mongolian peasant, and
the two British visitors had an unexpected opportunity to
make their acquaintance when the elevator became wedged
between two floors. They were eventually assisted out of the
elevator by some American reporters.

GBS seemed indefatigable—even after his long railroad
journey across Europe. Before lunch he insisted on seeing
the Lenin Mausoleum and the Kremlin, and the other members of the party were induced to tag along. Lady Astor was
greatly impressed by Lenin's vigorous profile. "A pure intellectual type—," Shaw assured her, "that is the true aristocracy . . . Henceforward Napoleon's tomb ranks second
instead of first." Later, when the party entered the Kremlin,
GBS gave the press photographers a piquant souvenir. With
a sprightly vault he launched himself astride one of the
Napoleonic cannons that had been captured in 1812. Cam-
eras clicked and Lady Astor smiled benignly, but showed
no willingness to emulate the seventy-four-year-old Shaw's
athletic prowess. The party now passed into the Council
Hall of the Soviet Congress. Shaw tried out the echo effects
but stopped abruptly when he overheard Nancy engaged in
a conversation about Marxism. "Remember," he said, re-
iterating one of his favorite comments, "I was a Marxist
almost before Lenin was born." He brushed aside Lady
Astor's remark that there was no real freedom of speech in
the Soviet Union by observing that the Russians were at
least "free from the illusion of democracy."

After lunch when the party visited the workers' Park of
Rest and Culture, GBS and Lady Astor, now arm in arm,
were still arguing about dialectical materialism. *Their* speech
was free enough, though it is impossible to say what the

Russians thought about it. As Lunacharsky had expected, Shaw did not confine his criticism to such aristocrats as Lady Astor. When someone pointed out a church that was soon to be demolished, GBS gratuitously advised the Russians to embark on a Five-Year aesthetic plan, adding, in mitigation, that "if a revolution like this had happened in America, England or France, they would have looted everything." At this Nancy cut short any further criticism of the West: "If you stand here soliloquizing we won't cover the ground."

That evening the party attended a special performance of Tairov's production of *The Beggar's Opera* at the Kamerny Theatre. Before the show began, the entire company marched on stage bearing a bright red banner which carried a dedication in English: "To the brilliant master, Bernard Shaw—a warm welcome to Soviet soil." Tairov then gave a brief speech of welcome to the British guests and Shaw was presented with a set of photographs of the Kamerny production of *Saint Joan*.

Next day, Lunacharsky's place was taken by Litvinov, the Soviet Commissar for Foreign Affairs, who escorted GBS on a visit to the Bolshoye Labor Commune, a reformatory center for criminals and juvenile delinquents. Shaw elaborates on his experiences in visiting this center in one particularly amusing section of "The Rationalization of Russia." Delinquency was evidently the special topic of the day, for GBS was later treated to a film show of *The Road to Life*, which dealt with the reform of young vagrants and criminals.

The program for the third day in Moscow included a morning tour of a highly efficient factory, the Electrozavod, where the Five-Year Plan had been accomplished in the record time of two and a half years. The British party inspected the plant in the company of the factory director,

and they were introduced to a group of workers who belonged to a literary circle. Shaw offered them more of his
gratuitous advice: "If you really work at the bench and do
not get away from the bench you will write well." Asked
to sign the visitors' book, he complied willingly, and added
a comment above his autograph: "My father drank too
much. I worked too much. Finish the Five-Year Plan in three
years and then take it easy."

As the party prepared to leave, all the factory workers
downed tools and rushed into the courtyard to cheer GBS.
A truckload of men drove up to the crowd and called for
a parting speech; whereupon Lady Astor asked to be allowed to say a few words. She was lifted onto the truck and
GBS was hoisted up after her. Then, with the aid of an
interpreter, she confronted her audience of Soviet shock
workers as confidently as if she were holding a pre-election
meeting in her own constituency. But mutterings of dis-
approval began as soon as she introduced herself as a British
capitalist and an aristocrat. Though she was a Conservative
she asked the workers to believe that she was really sym-
pathetic toward the U.S.S.R. "You have done some very
good things for which I am glad, and I hope you will go
from strength to strength. The Soviet Union must get in
step with the whole world and then the world will march
with you. While you have had great success, you are too
conceited."

One of the workers asked Lady Astor whether she would
prefer to live among British or Russian work people. "I
prefer the British," she replied. "The Russians have many
fine qualities, but they seem to be dreadfully meek. The
British proletarians have got guts, and will not be driven
like the Russians, even when it would be good for them."
Meekness was not evident in the angry roar that broke from

the crowd. "Who lives well?" they demanded, "The workers or the capitalists?" Heckling drowned Lady Astor's next few words as she raised her hand in a pacific gesture. Then, to the astonishment of everyone, GBS intervened: "The more I see of the proletarians the more I thank God I am not one."

When the gasp of astonishment died away several shock workers came forward and saluted Shaw. These men had been awarded the Order of Lenin for their outstanding production record. Shaw listened with interest to an account of their achievements and then offered them his congratulations. "In England," he said, "such privileged workers are not loved by the working masses. Here in Soviet Russia they are the most popular and are showered with honors by their fellow workers. Comrades, I am very glad to see such great enthusiasm here. When I return to England I shall try to persuade the English workers to do as you have done."

It was now the turn of the British Ambassador to act as host to his celebrated compatriots. At five in the afternoon, after paying a visit to Uzkoe, a scientists' rest home that had earned favorable comments from H. G. Wells, GBS and Lady Astor were received as guests of honor at a garden party in the grounds of the British Embassy. As the two celebrities arrived they were handed identical cablegrams from the United States. The message, from Dmitri Krynin, a professor of civil engineering at Yale, implored Lady Astor and GBS "in the name of humanitarian principles, please help my wife in Moscow." It was quickly ascertained that Krynin was a political exile who had fled from Russia and would be executed if he ever returned. His wife and family still lived in Moscow and the Russian authorities had refused to grant them permission to join Krynin in the United States. Litvinov was standing genially on the terrace when Lady Astor approached him with the telegram and suddenly knelt before him. Handing him the message she said, "I come before you as a peasant before a Czar. As in days of yore, I present a petition to your government on bended knee. Most humbly I pray you in the name of humanity to save this suffering family." Litvinov flushed and glanced hastily at the telegram. Then he thrust it back into her outstretched hands, his anger checked by his obvious embarrassment. "This matter is not within my jurisdiction," he muttered, and turned away.

A moment later the telegram was being scrutinized by reporters. They were overjoyed to discover that it mentioned Mrs. Krynin's address, and so, without further delay, they left the Embassy and sped through Moscow, descending en masse upon Mrs. Krynin's apartment. The bewildered woman knew nothing about the telegram and persistently refused to answer the reporters' questions. She was obviously terrified, by the relentless interrogation almost as much as by the sudden expectation of a visit from the G.P.U. Unfortunately her worst fears were soon to be realized.

Lady Astor, characteristically, would not take Litvinov's reaction as a final answer. At the Embassy it was suggested that the case should be brought before the political police. Whereupon GBS, Lady Astor, and Viscount Astor, accompanied by an Embassy attaché, drove off to the central office of the G.P.U. On Krynin's behalf Lady Astor badgered the Soviet police; she argued with government officials and raised the matter whenever she was sure of an audience of reporters. But all to no avail. The Russian authorities were more obdurate than Lady Astor, and they had their own way of dealing with the case. Soon after she had returned to England, reporters who tried to obtain another interview with Krynin's wife found that her apartment was occupied by a new tenant. The Krynin family had "disappeared."

However, the problem of an exile was not to be allowed to interfere with the itinerary. A two-day visit to Leningrad was next on the program. Early that same evening members of the British party were ushered aboard an express that carried them northward—to that city which, in 1917, had welcomed a very different exile as he leaped triumphantly from political obscurity to proclaim all power to the Soviets.

On the morning of July 24 the streets of Leningrad were thronged with sightseers; they had turned out in their thousands—not as enthusiastic Shavians but to catch a glimpse of the *Graf Zeppelin* as it proceeded en route to the Arctic Circle. Von Eckener, the German commander, was man of the hour, and on arrival the British party was immediately whisked off to an official reception in his honor. An hour or so later they were bundled into limousines and taken on a swift sight-seeing tour of the city. After lunch the pace was increased. GBS, a former art critic, remarked after a lightning tour of the Hermitage Art Galleries: "We marched past acres of pictures, but they all looked alike to me." He was then permitted to see the vaults in which were stored many unique treasures of gold and silver, but here he displayed even less interest than he had shown at the Hermitage. The first signs of Shavian enthusiasm occurred later in the day when the party was conducted on a tour of Tsarskoe Selo, the Children's Village. GBS now vied with Nancy Astor in questioning the children and their guardians and in discussing educational theories. It was beginning to dawn on some of the Russian guides that their foreign visitors were interested in people, in their problems and ideas, and not in museums and art galleries. This was what Shaw had meant when he spoke of coming to Russia for "serious business."

But the itinerary was, apparently, fixed and unalterable. Moscow provided the pattern for the tourist routine in Leningrad. First the sights of the city; then a tour of a model State institution, and finally, on the second day in Leningrad, a visit to the movies. For the second time in less than a week GBS sat through *The Road to Life;* then a few reels of *Battleship Potemkin* and *The End of St. Petersburg.*

Meanwhile, Lunacharsky had arrived. He had been invited by the Association of Proletarian Writers and Printers to act as chairman at a lunch in the Europa hotel in honor of Bernard Shaw. When GBS protested at the idea of meeting "more intellectuals" he was told that the members of the Association were not intellectuals. He chuckled and then admitted that this was quite true: writers were not really intellectuals—although he had always imagined that to be a trade secret. But if these writers were not intellectuals, what were they? Why, naturally, he was informed, they are the *intellectual proletariat.*

Most of the morning of July 25 was taken up with the making of a commemorative film which was shot at the request of Soyuzkino (Soviet Film Authority). The film became a "talkie" in which Lunacharsky made a brief introductory speech in praise of Shaw and then GBS made a long adulatory speech in praise of Lenin. He talked about Lenin and his achievements for nearly half an hour. "I'm sure they'll have to throw most of it away," he remarked as the cameramen were leaving. But he proved to be wrong. The film material was processed into a movie some 5,000 feet long, and when it was shown in Moscow five days later, GBS expressed surprise and satisfaction at its quality.

At last Shaw was beginning to show signs of fatigue. His lunch-reception at the Europa was followed by a rapid tour of St. Isaac's Cathedral; then he retired into the British

Embassy for a restful afternoon, emerging only once more, for a brief visit to the Anti-Religious Museum. Here a young girl who represented the League of the Godless showed him various exhibits that illustrated religious superstitions of the peasants. When they reached a case containing the undecayed corpses of two peasants, the girl knowledgeably explained how priests always maintained that such miracles of preservation happened only to saints. She was dumbfounded when Shaw instantly queried how she could be certain that the two muzhiks had not been saints. Earlier that day GBS had been even more directly critical of museums that exalted the memory of the revolutionists of Tsarist Russia. It was dangerous for the new regime to praise revolution now that all power had passed to the Soviets. He advised the authorities to get rid of all the exhibits of the revolutionary era and turn the museums into institutions of law and order.

Shaw rejoined the British party on the 11.30 train back to Moscow. Next day, July 26, 1931, would be his seventy-fifth birthday.

Soviet organizers could now sit back and wait for the spotlights to focus on the spectacular reception that awaited their guests in the Hall of Columns in the old Nobles' Club (Dom Soyuzov). During the late 'thirties the Hall of Columns acquired international notoriety as a showplace of Soviet justice. Birthday celebrations were to become far less frequent than treason trials, and receptions of a very different kind were held there for Bukharin and his associates in the case of the "anti-Soviet Trotskyite Center."

On this occasion the center of interest was not prosecutor and defendant, and the unexpected could still occur. From the moment when Shaw rose to reply to a vote of thanks, the vast audience in the Hall of Columns interrupted his speech with gasps of amazement. Many of the Russians were so astonished by his "asides" that the general import of his speech was lost on them. They were aghast at hearing how, before crossing the Soviet border, he had flung a supply of provisions out of the train because he was convinced that there were no food shortages in Russia. They were stupefied at his casual name-dropping. He referred to the patron saints of Communism as if they were his personal acquaintances: . . . "When I spoke to Engels. . . ." What was that? Did he say that he had spoken to Engels? Was it true that this Bernard Shaw had worked in the British Museum while Marx himself was there, writing *Das Kapital?* Lunacharsky could hardly have expected anything more consoling than Shaw's speech. GBS had come to eulogize Russia and every word that he uttered was worth a million rubles as propaganda. The most memorable Soviet words in response to Shaw's speech were contained in a letter from Maxim Gorky which was read aloud at Shaw's request:

Dear Bernard Shaw!
    Illness—angina—prevents me from coming to Moscow to warmly grasp your hand—the hand of a brave fighter and gifted man. You have lived three-fourths of a century, and with your sharp wit you have aimed countless destructive blows at the conservatism and insipidness of men. I rejoice to know that your seventy-fifth birthday is celebrated in a country which values you so highly, among people who have begun the mighty struggle with the world you scorn, and are carrying that struggle to victory.

The other British guests were less enthusiastic than Shaw; but then, of course, they were unrelenting capitalists. Lady Astor repaid Soviet hospitality by voicing her objections to the Russian custom of providing answers to questions that had not been asked, while ignoring questions that seemed inconvenient or embarrassing. Viscount Astor also had a disturbing fondness for asking awkward questions, but he kept his conclusions to himself. Worst of all was the Earl of Lothian, who maintained that Communism was a new kind of religious fanaticism that would culminate in war. Soviet developments, he claimed, were dominated by "war psychology." But good Communists knew when to close their ears, and, anyway, they had come to hear Bernard Shaw. These other foreigners were of little consequence.

That afternoon, for the first time in his life, Shaw somewhat reluctantly attended a race meeting, which he publicly described as "disgusting." He loathed horse-racing and was contemptuous of its survival as a sport in Soviet Russia. Before reaching the race-track he remarked to his guide, "I suppose there will be only one horse in the race, since there is no competition in a socialist State." Nevertheless, the race was being held in his honor and he was induced to present the prize to the winning jockey, who happened, by chance, to be a fellow Irishman. In *Who's Who?* GBS had declared his recreations to be "Anything but sport," and now the Muscovites, at least, could see that he was in earnest. Amid the excited roars of the crowd GBS fell asleep in his box while Nancy Astor fanned the flies from his face.

The whole of the following day, July 27, was spent in touring the nine-year-old Lenin Commune in the Kirsanovsky district of Moscow, where the British party was pleasantly surprised to encounter several English and American assistants. Guided by the head of the Commune, the visitors were shown every aspect of the social, cultural, and agricultural life of the community. Lady Astor, who was impressed by the entire organization, expressed particular interest in the nurseries and the children's quarters. Her outspoken comparisons of Soviet and British methods of child care were soon to lead to the despatch of a Russian study group to England, where they could examine British methods at first hand. Lady Astor's special interest in child welfare, which had already been in evidence at the Tsarskoe Selo in Leningrad, was to come to the fore again during her interview with Stalin.

Next day, as a deliberate contrast to the commune, the party was taken to Ira, a village which had not yet organized a collective. Here they were invited to mingle with the reactionary peasants, to meet the superstitious village priest, and then draw inevitable conclusions about the advantages of the commune system.

Their conclusions, if any, were overshadowed by the momentous meetings of July 29. In the afternoon GBS and Lady Astor called on Maxim Gorky at his cottage in a small village just outside Moscow. Then, at eight in the evening, accompanied by Viscount Astor, Lord Lothian, Litvinov, and a British Foreign Office interpreter, they were solemnly ushered into the presence of Stalin and remained with him for two hours and ten minutes. Unfortunately, there are no available verbatim reports of either of these meetings, although on subsequent occasions GBS and Lady Astor were to make piecemeal allusions to the substance of their interview with the Soviet leader.

At 10.30 the visitors' cars drew up outside the Metropole. When Shaw stepped out he was immediately surrounded by newspapermen asking for details of the interview with Stalin. He smiled broadly and began to make his way through the crowd without replying. Hopefully, the reporters trailed into the hotel, where, just before he disappeared from sight behind the elevator doors, GBS turned to them and remarked, "He has a black moustache."

The other members of the party were equally laconic. The

press had to remain satisfied with the information that it had been "a most enjoyable occasion." Even the Soviet news agencies evidently received no details of the interview. Western news commentators were convinced that the British party had not given a pledge to remain silent about the interview, but it was felt that the British Foreign Office might in some way be accountable for the uncooperative attitude of the visitors. Perhaps an official statement was being prepared: certainly the party had been accompanied by a Foreign Office representative, and this lent some credence to the possibility. But within a few days it became evident that there would be no official communiqué about the meeting. Presumably the visitors had remained silent because of their personal intentions of capitalizing on the unique newsworthiness of the interview. There would be no reports until GBS and Lady Astor returned to England and wrote the inevitable books about Russia.

A few persistent reporters who remained at the Metropole were surprised at the reappearance of the party in the hotel lounge. Before midnight, quite unexpectedly, the visitors drove off to Moscow's only "night club," where they enjoyed a hearty meal and were entertained by gypsy singers and dancers.

July 30 was Shaw's last day in Moscow. It was bound to be something of an anticlimax, although it lacked neither the variety nor the pace of the previous nine days.

At breakfast in the Metropole Litvinov took the opportunity to reply to the criticism of the British aristocrats. He freely admitted that many Soviet ideas were not original to Communist Russia, but insisted in defense that the greatness of the Soviet Union was demonstrated in the willingness of her people to learn from anyone. The Western news correspondents found Shaw's response unashamedly adulatory.

GBS declared that the ideas now being implemented in the U.S.S.R. were the expression of the greatest minds of all the ages. "But," he added, "the great difference lies in this, that you brought these ideas to life, and that when any new, advanced ideas come to you, the whole government apparatus, all its organs, the press and society get down to realizing these ideas, while in England, every advanced idea is met not with sympathy, but with furious opposition by the Government and the press."

Later that morning Shaw saw the film he had made in Leningrad. He also spent several hours listening to cases at the People's Court and was fascinated by the authoritative self-assurance of the women judges. In the afternoon, while Lord Lothian and Viscount Astor visited the October Red Army Camp, GBS and Lady Astor were taken at their own request to see Madame N. K. Krupskaya, Lenin's widow, whom Shaw found to be a most lovable person despite the fact that she was one of the two ugliest women in Europe (the other was Mrs. William Booth of the Salvation Army). The itinerary concluded after dinner with a visit to the All-Russian Cooperative Art Society, which was presenting an exhibition of paintings by S. Koltsov.

Shaw was now ready to make an official statement to the Western press representatives in Moscow. Toward dusk reporters gathered in the lobby of the Metropole to hear his general impressions of Russia and to learn how the visit had affected his attitude to Communism generally and to the U.S.S.R. in particular. GBS left them in no doubt that Russia was all right and the Western powers were all wrong. "I am more than ever convinced," he said, "that I was right when I warned capitalist nations that they must adopt Russia's methods if they would escape collapse. I had no idea Russia had gone so far." When a correspondent reminded Shaw of

H. G. Wells's warning that the Soviet system might fall because of its lack of managerial talent and its inadequate civil service, GBS responded with a vigorous attack on all critics of the Soviet regime. "In all prophecies of Russia's failure, the wish is father to the thought. I do not know why any human being who desires the social welfare of humanity should wish the experiment to fail. But we have a lot of foolish people who do want it to fail. They may take it from me that it is not going to do so." To dispel any lingering doubts about his impressions of the U.S.S.R., Shaw then wrote a parting testimonial in the Metropole Visitors' Book. "There is not a more interesting country in the world today to visit than Soviet Russia, and I find travelling there perfectly safe and pleasant. . . . To be in a country where there are no ladies or gentlemen but everyone is a friend is as rare as it is refreshing . . . Tomorrow I leave this land of hope and return to our Western countries of despair."

At midnight the British party bade farewell to their Russian hosts and boarded the express for Warsaw. Bernard Shaw had come and gone; but *his* ten days had not shaken the Russian world.

Several months later the U.S.A. was given the exclusive honor of a radio broadcast by GBS. It was beamed from the B.B.C. in London and rebroadcast over the Columbia radio network. Shaw's speech, entitled "Look, You Boobs," was intended to put the Americans right about Russia. (The "boobs" were the Americans.) But as a propagandist Shaw was not conspicuously successful either in his broadcasting or later, in 1933, when he spoke in person at New York's Metropolitan Opera House. Even earlier he had abandoned his "Rationalization of Russia," the affirmation through direct experience of his faith in the new regime.

GBS was, self-confessedly, a political failure according to

his own standards. "The successful man," he observed, "is one who has people doing what he wants them to do. But they're always doing what I don't want them to." This deep sense of frustrating noninvolvement, evident even behind his mask of confident assertions about the U.S.S.R., is perhaps the fundamental reason for Shaw's abandonment of what might have been his most formidable attempt at a rationalization of Russia.

HARRY M. GEDULD

Indiana University
October, 1963

BERNARD SHAW

Shaw in Leningrad. *Front row left to right:* Karl Radek, M. Lunacharsky, Lady Astor, Bernard Shaw, M. Chalatov. *Standing, left to right:* Lidia Seifullina, writer; Bela Illesi, writer; Vsevolod Ivanov (with glasses).

UPI

Shaw and his secretary, Blanche Patch

Baron Studios

EDITOR'S NOTE

Except for obvious typing and punctuation errors, the published text of *The Rationalization of Russia* conforms to the original manuscript, retaining Shaw's idiosyncrasies of punctuation and orthography. All corrected readings have been indicated in footnotes.

I should like to thank Miss E. Barber of the Society of Authors, Mr. T. S. Pattie (British Museum), Miss Miriam S. Farley, Mr. Richard V. Hughes, Mr. Dan H. Laurence, and the Chief Librarian of Buxton for their assistance in the preparation of this book. I must also express my gratitude to the late Dean Ralph L. Collins of Indiana University, without whose encouragement *The Rationalization of Russia* might never have been published. My greatest indebtedness is to my parents, to whom my editorial efforts are dedicated.

H.M.G.

The Rationalization of Russia

Preface

Most of what is current today in England and America about Communist Russia is written by persons who should never have been taught to write, and read by people who should never have been taught to read. For these accomplishments are as dangerous in the hands of the uneducated as a stick of dynamite in the hands of a baby. And today we are worse than uneducated: we are miseducated. Mr H. G. Wells understated the case when he complained that Gladstone, a typical product of public school and university education, was grossly ignorant.[1] If he had been, his natural mental power and character would have enabled him to learn easily all that he needed to know. But he began his political life with every corner of his mind so carefully stuffed with pernicious rubbish: tribal superstitions imposed on him as religion; glorifications of piracy, brigandage, slave-trading, and murder disguised as history; excuses for robbery, idleness, and mad pride labelled as political economy; and dishonest slacking and shirking of social duty idolized as liberty, that when he became Chancellor of the Exchequer he declared that England's prosperity was increasing by

leaps and bounds when it was in fact a feebly palliated hell
for nine-tenths of the population, whilst the rest were wasting the plunder of the poor in digging their graves with
their teeth, not having been taught even how to feed and
clothe themselves healthily. A grossly ignorant person would
have been a far safer leader of the nation; for he (or she)
might have done the right thing by accident or sheer naïveté,
whereas though Gladstone never said to himself "Evil, be
thou my good", yet having been carefully trained by his
upbringing and schooling to mistake evil for good, his condition came to the same thing in an incurable form. That
is why our Cabinets, consisting of men of unchallenged respectability, and often of the best intentions, are in effect
Cabinets of scoundrels, and why our bishops, who always
have a saint or two among them as well as a blackguard or
two, are at best in the position of chaplains to a pirate
fleet. The corruption of a predatory society cannot be cured
by reforms within that form of society: it is fundamental;
and the remedy is the revolutionary one of a complete substitution of systematically enforced honesty for systematically encouraged predacity.

In our predaceous society, politely called by my friend
Mr Tawney an acquisitive society,[2] the Press invariably
shares and voices the fundamental corruption. Its business
is to hold a candle to the devil by flattering predacity and
representing constitutional honesty as execrable villainy.
This is the explanation of the Anti-Sovietism of the British
and American newspapers, and consequently of the millions
whose opinions are formed by them. I do not write this
book with any intention of converting these good people.
They will be converted exactly as they have been perverted.
The day will come when their newspapers will say different
things, as will their nurses and teachers; and their minds will

be changed accordingly without any trouble to themselves.
I am writing now as a revolutionist to revolutionists in the
light of the accomplished revolution in Russia. I have often
before written as a Socialist to Socialists; but Socialism
means no more now than Christianity meant after its acceptance by Constantine: events have proved that we can
have Governments of professed Socialists under Socialist
Prime Ministers without the slightest constitutional change.
Socialism is actually derided by the up-to-date young as a
back number: a nineteenth century Fabian fad that is no
longer in fashion. Social-Democracy, which in the days of
Bismarck and Gladstone was the extreme Left in politics, is
now the extreme Right of the bourgeois Left, and the recog-
nized Opposition to Communism. We hear of Social-revolu-
tionaries of the Right and of the Left, all classed as enemies
by the Communists. The Ultra-Red Socialists of yesterday:
Hyndman, Kantsky [Kautsky], Miliukoff, Kerensky,[3] figure
in the newest Russian polemics as imperialist reactionaries
and bourgeois democrats, the last epithet being the most
contemptuous of all.

Placid ladies and gentlemen who still classify the political
world into Conservatives, Liberals, and rag tag and bobtail
who have no business in it at all, are not conscious of this
confusion. To them Socialism seems a perfectly solid and
homogenous [sic] sediment of wickedness and folly: consequently all Socialists are alike to them. But to the Socialists
themselves—and common political thought has slipped much
further into Socialism than it knows—the change of values,
and the consequent new orientations of vituperation, are
very puzzling; for all these people: Fabians, Social-democrats, Right and Left Social Revolutionaries, Labor Party
Left wings, and Communists, are Socialists, or at least think
they are. They all believe in public control of industry for

the common good, public ownership of the sources of production and the machinery of exchange, and public education of all children in the principles of Communism, including the inculcation of the belief that living by private ownership is simply a legalized method of theft. And when they say public they mean proletarian. In short, they are all fundamentally opposed to our Capitalist system, and contemptuous of its pretences to honesty, respectability, and piety.

How, then, has it happened that now that all their wildest hopes have been realised by the sudden transformation of the most backward of the European empires into a federation of Communist republics in which the advocacy of private property is high treason, they all, instead of finding themselves a happy family, come to loggerheads so fiercely that every section except one finds itself in the old Tsarist position of being in opposition to a Government which tolerates no opposition?

The answer is that it is possible to be a strongly convinced Socialist, and have cordial dislike of bourgeois society without any provision of the forms of government which Communism in practice will irresistibly create and impose. We cannot smash Capitalism without smashing its institutions; and its institutions include not only its predatory and oppressive organs but the defensive, humanitarian, palliative and popular brakes and checks and safeguards and franchises and "liberties" which it has consented to partly in fear of rebellion and partly in a natural recoil from its own worst villainy in pursuit of profits. And when Communism makes a clean sweep of the lot, Socialists who have spent their lives upholding [,] volunteering for these forlorn hopes and manning (and womanning) these bulwarks are horrified and often driven into flat reaction, never having reflected that when the Bastille has been stormed and demolished the

orientations of vituperation, are very puzzling; for all these people:
Fabians,Social-democrats,Right and Left Social Revolutionaries,Labor
Party Left wings,and Communists,are Socialists, or at least think they
are. They all believe in public control of industry for the common good,
public ownership of the sources of production xf and the machinery of
exchange,and public education of all children in the principles of Communism,
including the inculcation of the belief that living by private ownership
is simply a legalized method of theft. And when they say public they
mean proletarian. In short, they are all fundamentally opposed to our
Capitalist system,and contemptuous of its pretences to honesty,respectability,and piety.

How,then,has it happened that now that all their wildest hopes have
been realised by the sudden transformation of the most backward of the
European empires into a federation of Communist republics in which the
advocacy of private property is high treason,they all,instead of finding
themselves a happy family,come to loggerheads so fiercely that every
section except one finds itself in the old Tsarist position of being in
opposition to a Government which tolerates no opposition?

The answer is that it is possible to be a strongly convinced Socialist,and have cordial dislike of bourgeois society without any pre-
vision of the forms of government which Communism in practice will
irresistibly create and impose. We cannot smash Capitalism without
smashing its institutions; and its institutions include not only its predatory and
offensive organs but the defensive, humanitarian, palliative and popular
brakes and checks and safeguards and "liberties" which it has consented to partly in
fear of rebellion and partly in a natural recoil from its own worst villainy in pursuit
of profits. And when Communism makes a clean sweep of the lot, Socialists who have
spent their lives upholding and manning (and womanning) these bulwarks

regulations for the protection * of his prisoners are no longer needed, and survive only as superstitions in the minds of the disbanded warders. For the thousandth time I have to note how hard superstitions die: how easy it is to induce people to adopt new ideas and how desperately difficult it is to induce them to scrap the old ones which the new have exploded. When I think of all the time and work I have wasted on parliamentary elections, for instance: the crowds that have come to hear me calling on them to vote for Tweedledum against Tweedledee and practising all the arts of the platform on them until they rose and sang "For he's a jolly good fellow" in a transport of delusion in which they seemed to themselves to be really doing something of intense political importance [.]

But this is not the case with revolutionary Communism. That is now a working reality, purged of all its old follies and adulterations; and the purpose of this book is to describe and explain this purgation by trial and error, as we shall no doubt go through it all ourselves as the penalty of our incapacity for learning from experience. Before getting to business let me make one statement of the general position.

About three-quarters of a century ago, a German Jew in exile in London, by name Karl Marx, published an epoch-making description and criticism of our capitalist system in which, after producing the necessary moral shock by shewing from our own official documents the atrocity of the system in its bearings on the huge proletarian majority of the nation, he proceeded to shew that the system had in its own nature and logic the seeds of its own disruption and dissolution. Though he lived most respectably with his wife and daughters at an unexceptionable address at Haverstock Hill,

* MS. has] protedtion.

and was buried in Highgate Cemetery where his tomb is still visited by pious pilgrims, he was at once classed as an emissary of the devil, and took the place on the capitalist index occupied a century earlier by Voltaire, Rousseau, and Tom Paine, and in the Middle Ages by "the accurst Mahound."

Time passed; but the capitalist system shewed no signs of cracking up as Marx had prophesied: on the contrary it went from miracle to miracle in productive power, and the financiers who had thought in thousands in Marx's day now thought in millions, whilst the "surplus value" impetticosed by those who preyed on society instead of producing for it, piled up outrageously. And so Marx became a back number.

Then another prophet of evil arose: this time no German Jew exile and political suspect, but a professor of unimpeachable credentials, whose hobby was extinct civilizations. This academic ghoul [4]—if he will forgive me for calling him so—dug up no less than six civilizations of which we had never so much as heard, and coolly informed us in a convincing manner that they were just like our own, and when they had reached the stage at which the social symptoms tallied with those now being exhibited in the centre of the British Empire, had dissolved and left not a wrack behind [5] in the fashion adumbrated by Shakespear and specified by Karl Marx.

The thoughtful few now felt that this was becoming serious; but our statesmen, who never read anything but the newspapers and had no time to think, continued to assume that capitalist civilization, rooted in laboriously inculcated human vices (which they called human nature), is immortal and eternal, and went on as before, although they noticed that the old machine was requiring a great deal of patching and repairs of a kind dangerously inconsistent with its original design.

Still, they went on gaily enough until, having let their foreign policies relapse into the hands of the militarists, they suddenly found themselves up to the neck in a stupendous war, the upshot of which was that Germany, without being at the least disadvantage in point of fighting and military glory, found herself starved out and for the moment obliged to sue for mercy. The victors, not understanding that Germany is a vital organ of the international capitalism to which they all belong, and that her destruction must involve their own, proceeded at once to plunder her as recklessly and vindictively as if they were buccaneers and she a merchantman who had infuriated them by putting up a stiff fight and killing a good many of them. In spite of the clearest warnings from the few people who knew what they were talking about and were studying the figures whilst the others were wallowing in their gratified war passions, the victors demanded not only a ruinous ransom from Germany but more than she could possibly pay. And they got out of that difficulty by lending her the money to pay it. This silly game did not last very long. When Germany could borrow no more she could pay neither the instalments of the ransom nor the interest on the money she had borrowed to stave them off. This put the victorious allies into Queer Street; for they had borrowed money for the war from England; and England had borrowed it from America; and they were depending on the German ransom to pay the interest on these huge debts. When Germany defaulted there was nothing for it but to face the facts and wipe the slates all round; but they had not the nerve to do this; and when they were at last convinced that the ransom neither would

nor could be paid, announced with an air of magnanimity
and a big word, moratorium, that they would wait a year
for it. They did; and found themselves just where they were
before. So they prolonged the moratorium, and will have to
keep on prolonging it until the Day of Judgment; for any
attempt to enforce payment of the ransom would drive Germany to flat repudiation, possible by a revolutionary government.

Meanwhile, the Bank of England, presuming on the ransom, had lent money for long terms throughout Europe to
such an extent that when the ransom dried up it was obliged
to borrow for short terms to meet its immediate engage-
ments. The moratorium created a financial panic throughout Europe; the bank's creditors were alarmed; there was a
European run on it; and the Bank of England broke. But
as the shutters did not go up, and business continued as
usual at from thirteen to fifteen shillings to the pound, the
crash was disguised by an auriferous phrase. It was called
"going off the gold standard".

Unfortunately, in a desperate but quite unintelligent attempt to save the Bank at the last moment, this going off
the gold standard had been held up *in terrorem* to the nation as the most horrible calamity that could befal[1] a
nation; and we were called on to submit patriotically to a
general reduction in wages and increase in taxation, and,
incidentally, to a Coalition Government, to save it. We submitted; and immediately the gold standard was not only repudiated but its repudiation was announced as a signal
benefit to the community and a stimulus to the revival of
trade. Brazen impudence and technical ignorance could go
no further. But the British Public, short as its memory is and
Cimmerian as its darkness and bewilderment in matters of
currency and finance as distinguished from individual busi-

ness practice, could not help wondering how the national perdition of Tuesday could become the national salvation of Friday when nothing had happened between but a general election.

This gold business requires a word of explanation. Our statesmen spoke of going off the gold standard exactly as if the officers of a sinking ship in mid ocean had said "Dont be alarmed: all we have to do is to get off the ship." And no-one was intelligent enough to say "Get off whither? Into the sea?" What is important on such occasions is not the standard you are going off from, but the one you are going on to. Your currency, when it ceases to represent one valuable commodity must represent some other, or group of others; else nobody will accept it. If you withdraw your promise to pay in gold without at once promising to pay in something else you must go back to simple barter. There will be an interval during which your bills of exchange and the like will be discounted on the chance that you will be able to pay in meal or in malt; but presently you will have either to (a) make a new standard based on a group of commodities valued by an index number, (b) conduct your trade by barter, or (c) return to the gold standard.

The objection to the gold standard is that though gold is valuable everywhere, it is not producible everywhere, and can therefore be cornered, hoarded, and monopolized. A land may be flowing with milk and honey (or water power) and crammed with baser metals and minerals, and yet, if it must pay its debts in gold, be made bankrupt by States which either have gold mines or have cornered the available supply of gold and are sitting on it.

Now when the German ransom business began, Germany admittedly could not pay in gold, because she had none. When she was allowed, and indeed ordered, to pay in ships, the shipyards on the Tees, the Tyne, and the Clyde found their occupation gone, their workers unemployed, and their owners ruined. The ships had to be hastily countermanded. The mere suggestion that payments should be made in steel brought a threat of rebellion from the British steelsmelters. Coal was worse. South Wales was already on the dole because Germany was sending to France for nothing, as pure plunder, the supplies she had formerly bought from British collieries. Our Prime Minister demanded payment in potash; but if there had been potash enough on earth to pay the ransom, England was not prepared to live on potash for thirty years. In the end, Germany, it appeared, must manage to buy gold and pay with it; and her creditors must pay England in gold, and England must pay America in gold. Gold flowed into America until she had more than she knew what to do with; so she simply hoarded it and thereby made it useless as currency; for the whole theory of gold money rests on the assumption that gold is a commodity in free general use and circulation. France, though some of the gold was pouring into her coffers, was the first of the victors to declare herself bankrupt. She also found a big word for it: Stabilization; but the fact was that she repudiated eighty percent of her war debts by taking her tenpenny franc off the gold standard and replacing it thereon at two-pence. Finally France managed to corner all the gold that was not being hoarded in America; and the Bank of England, not being able to procure gold enough to pay its debts, broke as aforesaid.

Now the bitter humor of the situation was that all this bankruptcy was produced, not by the losses of the Allies, but by their ill-gotten gains. For America, after draining Europe of its gold, crashed more sensationally than any of them, and had such budget deficits and millions of unemployed that her plight was more pitiable than Germany's.

At the bottom of all this welter of solvent insolvency, there were two main mistakes which may be called commercial complexes. First, it was assumed that what was going on was trade. Second, it was assumed that trade in itself was a desirable thing, and that without trade nothing could be done and nations must starve helplessly. Neither of these propositions will hold water. The payments made by Germany are not trade: they are tribute. And the payments of interest on investments are not trade: they also are a tribute paid by labor to land and capital for the right to exist. Trade means exchange of goods and services, imports paid for by exports and exports by imports, beneficial to both parties, a fair exchange being no robbery. Where there is payment without exchange, all on one side, the transaction, whatever its legal name may be, and for whatever reasons it may be tolerated, has all the economic effects of robbery, and the moral ones too. I keep bees and provide my breakfast table with honey by robbing them of all the honey they produce save what they must retain to keep them alive. But this is not trade; and when I receive dividends from my foreign investments, they do not give rise to trade with foreigners: I rob them as I rob the bees. The fact that years ago, I, or somebody from whom I have bought the power to exact this tribute, sent enough money abroad to support a body of workers whilst they were making a railway or digging a mine or building and equipping a factory or the like has no more to do with present trade than the fact that my beehives and artificial honeycombs cost me a few pounds say ten years ago creates trade between me and the bee.

Now all of us who have acquired more money than we need spend by applying the bee process to our own compatriots have been investing hundreds of millions of that

spare money abroad as long as you or I can remember, and
for many lifetimes before that too. If you take the enormous
tribute resulting from this; pile on top of it the enormous
ransom imposed on Germany; and persist in reckoning it
as trade and applying the economics of trade to the solution
of the problems it gives rise to, you will presently find your-
self in an unholy mess, which is precisely where our statesmen and financiers and bankers are. And if, further, the
tribute gets divided into reparations for damage done, of
which France, having suffered most of the damage, takes
the lion's share, and the rest goes to America as interest on
the money borrowed from her for the war, and if again the
pauperization of the workers and ruin of industries brought
upon countries by receiving tributes instead of money honestly earned, forces them to bargain for payment in gold instead of miscellaneous commodities, then obviously America
will automatically corner all the gold that is not cornered by
France; and both of them have so much more than they
can use that they will wallow in it helplessly like the giant
Fafnir in the Niblung [6] legend whilst the Bank of England
breaks for lack of gold, and similar bankruptcies, with Stock
Exchange closings, moratoriums, and the like, are occurring
all over the commercial world.

The remedy seems ridiculously easy. Why does not the
Bank of England buy gold from France and America with
commodities? Simply because America refuses to have the
commodities dumped on her to the ruin of her industries
and the spread of an already crushing unemployment. Every
attempt to buy gold with goods is met by a prohibitive tariff.

In the deadlock thus created we naturally say to America
"Well, if you refuse to be paid in the only way we can pay
you, had you not better cry off the debt?" And we say the
same thing to France. And both America and France in-

stantly shriek simultaneously "What! Forego our just dues and let you cheat us!" They will have to all the same because the deadlock is only the practical expression of the eternal natural fact that nations in so far as they are not wholly self-sufficing, must live by honest trade and not by military plunder and human bee-keeping in any of its forms. For the gods must be laughing very heartily at these terrestrial beggars on horseback vowing to deluge the world in blood again if they are not paid to the uttermost farthing, and then, when their perfectly solvent debtors rush to pay and over-pay, scatter them with volleys of tariffs so meticulous that a woman cannot cross a frontier without the risk of being arrested for smuggling her hairpins.

The other delusion—that trade is a good thing in itself—turns all our city articles and commercial forecasts into fairy tales and foolishness. Trade is of course good business for the trader just as murder is good business for the executioner. But in itself it is simply a cost of distribution to be reduced, like other costs, as far as possible. When trade is at its maximum, the trader thinks it is at its optimum, though from the point of view of the consumer it is at its pessimum. The ideal is to have production and consumption within immediate reach of one another. Let me make this clear by an illustration which I have used again and again without being able to find a more effective one for bible-reading countries.

Ask any typical city editor to report on the condition of the Garden of Eden in its first year. His first care will be to ascertain the balance of trade by carefully computing and comparing the exports and imports. To his horror he will find that there are no exports, no imports, no balance of trade because there is no trade. He will report that the condition of the Garden is desperate, and that his stock remedy of a reduction in the Bank Rate is not available because there is no bank except the one on which the wild thyme grows. The speedy death from starvation of Adam and Eve will be declared inevitable as long as Eve persists in plucking apples from the tree and Adam in immediately eating them.

Let us next suppose that Adam and Eve, through eating the fruit of the Tree of Knowledge (symbolizing a university education) are impressed by the city editor[']s report, and, to save themselves from their prophesied doom, take to trade, Eve, instead of handing the apple to her hungry husband, sells it to a Persian fruit wholesaler, who sells it to a middleman, who sells it to another middleman, who sells it to an Afghan dealer, who sells it to a middleman, who sells it to another middleman, who sells it to a speculator, who sells it to an Indian, starting from whom it reaches successively Thibet, China, Manchuria, Japan, San Francisco, Vancouver, Montreal, London, Paris, Alexandria, Jerusalem, Baghdad, where it is sold to a firm specializing in expensive foreign fruits by whom it is sold in an almost uneatable and wholly innutritious condition to Adam at a price which must cover all its travelling expenses plus the commissions of the middlemen and the profits of the exporters in addition to a handsome profit for the Baghdad retailers.

The city editor, called on by Adam for a further report, would now declare that by an unprecedented extension of its foreign trade the Garden of Eden had been raised from an apparently hopeless state of moribund penury to a flourishing prosperity in which the shares of its fruit exporting companies might be regarded as his selection for the week of a particularly attractive investment. The simple facts would be a high death rate from eating rotten or icekilled fruit, and a grievous addition to the burden of labor needed to obtain even that deleterious refreshment.

This senseless cry of trade when there is no trade, and prosperity when things are getting dearer, has muddled us until we can no longer be dealt with as rational creatures; but that does not prevent some of us from being imposingly clever and ready with figures within the limits of our delusion. The unskilled public are dumb in the presence of experts whom they suppose to be starting from the general agreement that two and two make four, though they are really assuming that two minus four makes six.

These experts are far more dangerous than their nineteenth century predecessors, because the separation between industry and finance was not then nearly so complete as it has since become. When the industrialists had to finance their own concerns they knew that they had to deal with commodities, and that money was only a measure of their value. But today a financier knows nothing of commodities, having never been down a mine nor made a factory. He thinks in figures exclusively. And finally figures cease to represent even money to him: they represent credit; and he comes to believe that great industries are built of credit and not of bricks and mortar, machines and men, clothes, houses, and provisions. He believes that the war was fought on credit instead of on bully beef, trinitrotoluene, khaki clothing, steel and blood, and that the millions of dead were slain by bills of exchange and war loan scrip instead of by shells and bayonets. A quite able and earnest American man of business sent me a book containing a carefully thought out plan for paying for the war in I forget how many years painlessly. He did not know that wars have to be paid for on the nail, and that though those who find the money may do so in consideration of their being allowed to tax the future earnings of the nation until they too are repaid on the nail or have the debt extinguished politely by taxation or summarily by repudiation, the war is paid for and done and gone, and their money with it. Yet because their claim to be repaid an equivalent sum remains on record at the Bank of England, the bankers come to think that the money is there as well as the written figure; and grave statisticians count it[,] under the heading Capital, as an actual part of the nations's [sic] wealth: an asset instead of a liability.

The bankers who take care of our money for us only that they may make profits by lending it out, and are therefore creditors by profession, have lost all sense of men and things, and live in an imaginary world of credit. Now real credit is only the banker[']s opinion that if he gives (say) a woman a pint of milk, she will return the compliment presently by giving him a pint and a tablespoonful; and though what the woman or her baby consumes is not his opinion but actual milk from the cow, he comes to believe that as the woman has not only got the milk from him but the credit, the transaction, in terms of credit, represents two pints instead of one. Schemes for the financial regeneration of the country by "utilizing credit" (which means drinking non-existent milk) have been put before the country and been seriously discussed, and either advocated enthusiastically or rejected with portentous earnestness for every reason on earth except the simple and obvious one that they are blazing nonsense.

Now the appalling mess in which we have been bogged by this illusion of banking and stock exchange practice, and by the general contempt for scientific reasoning, is making many of us cry that Professor Flinders Petrie and Karl Marx were right, and that Capitalism is played out. That is not quite so. Karl Marx did not say that Capitalism would break up because the silly capitalists did not know their own silly business. Professor Flinders Petrie did not criticise Capitalism: he only told us what had hitherto invariably happened to it. Our modern realistic historians refuse to join the general scare caused by the mess: they say, in effect, that there is nothing new in Capitalism being in a mess, as the beastly thing has always been in a mess, more or less. Messes can be cleaned up; and the fact that we never do clean them up until they do us so much harm, and threaten to do so much more, that it is physically and morally impossible to keep on making them worse, does not exclude [sic] the possibility of our cleaning up this one when we absolutely have to or perish. Without abandoning the Capitalist state we can for the moment wipe the slate of the war debt and the reparations and the unconditional annuities, and all the rest of it. We can discard the gold standard and substitute commodity standards grouped under index numbers. We can get rid of the fluctuation of foreign exchange by a managed international currency. We can abolish unnecessary trade by absolute prohibition of imports of the goods we had better produce for ourselves. We can make necessary trade free trade. We can steal a few tricks from Socialism by nationalizing banking, transport, mining, and power supply, and organizing and controlling collective agriculture. We can reform and reconstruct our government machinery, and get sufficient effectual national control of industry to put an end to the present irresponsibility of purely venal private enterprise. I do not say that we shall have character enough or are teachable enough to do these things in the teeth of the bankers and billbrokers and shipowners and their retinues who live by foreign trade and domestic money-lending, and in whose hands our Cabinets have all the helplessness of

technical ignorance. I do not know whether Professor Flinders Petrie can produce any archaeological evidence that
the extinct civilizations ever prolonged their agony in this
manner. The historians have exploded the old legend that
the Roman Empire was assegaied summarily by barbarians
tobogganing down the Alps on their shields like Buxton
schoolboys on tea trays: [7] it seems to have been simple bankruptcy, financial and moral, and not a rejuvenating and
easily absorbed immigration of outlandish folk that made
an end of it. But I think our pessimists and catastrophists are
hasty in thinking that the hour has arrived when the tremendous strain set up by competitive private capitalism
has reached explosion point, and that the present deadlock
is an impasse. The strains can still be relieved or shifted
sufficiently to be bearable whilst the psychology of the
masses is still capitalistic and nationalistic. Much as they
have to bear they have borne worse before; and it is their
hope and not their despair that capitalism has to dread, if
indeed that dread does not itself turn to hope and the capitalists become enlightened enough to will their own destruction as such: a state of mind which I share with the best of
my contemporaries.

I shall therefore not treat the present situation as a ful-
filment of the forecast of Marx. The change from Capitalism
to Communism has not come about as he predicted. It has
been established in one State with Capitalism in full swing
in all the other States. It has been established not in the
most but in the least industrial State. It has been opposed by
most of the doctrinaire Marxists. And the revolutionary situation which made it possible has been the accident of a
foolish war produced by the assassination of an Archduke,
not the culmination of a phase of social evolution. It was
something that might happen anywhere, anyhow, instead

of under the conditions laid down by Marx. The theory that
a revolution cannot take place until there is a revolutionary
situation, though it is one of the Marxist affectations, and
is a convenient excuse for the large number of revolutionists
who dread the revolution their principles oblige them to
make, loses some of its apparent profundity in view of
Marx's demonstration that under Capitalism there is always a revolutionary situation. All that can be said for it is
that the inertia of an established State is so enormous that
as long as the masses receive enough to keep them in the
station of life to which they are accustomed, and the armed
retainers of the State are paid punctually, a catastrophic
revolution is impracticable unless it is deliberately desired
and contrived by the Government itself as in the case of the
Japanese change from Feudalism to Capitalism, or as a mere
dynastic revolution desired by the governing class, like the
revolution which substituted the House of Hanover for
the House of Stuart on the British throne.[8] Even the French
Revolution, in which the proletariat was only the catspaw
of the bourgeoisie, might have been suppressed if the monarchy had been a capable one and the soldiers' wages paid
up instead of being several years in arrear[s]. Dictators'
coups d'etat, and palace revolutions, in which the controllers
of the governmental forces and machinery are ousted violently by a new set, are not revolutions in the Marxian sense,
and are very unstable if they produce no other change.

A revolution in a highly developed industrial State is extremely difficult because of the absolute dependence of the
people on a complicated machinery which they do not understand and cannot work except under specialized direc-
tion and management. The old fable of the rebellion of the
limbs against the belly has more point in modern times than
it had in the mouth of Menenius.[9] A ferryman with a boat

and a pair of oars can snap his fingers at organized society; and the village blacksmith can look the whole world in the face; but a sailor in a modern battleship or an assembler in an automobile factory is by himself much more helpless than a baby, who knows quite well where to clutch and how to suck for its subsistence. An Italian friend of mine who conducted a marine engineering establishment was informed by his men one day that they were syndicalists; that henceforth the factory belonged to them on the syndicalist principle of the factory to the factory hands, the mine to the miners, the railway to the railway workers and so forth; and that he had better clear out. He did so. A week later they came to him and told him to clear in again, as they could make nothing of the business.

Now this difficulty does not occur in a backward agricultural country cultivated by peasants. If they seize the land they can make something out of it. They may reduce big farms, ably managed and skilfully cultivated, to miserable strips which return a wretched living to incessant and brutalizing toil; but they do not find themselves in one day without artificial light, without driving power, without food, without water, and without the faintest notion how to set the supplies going again. The primitive peasant who has land has everything he is conscious of needing: the urban proletarian has nothing unless he has the co-operation of thousands of mates and a hierarchy of managers, mathematicians, chemical experts, designers, inventors, and technical specialists of all kinds, themselves co-operating with specialists in marketing, transport, and heaven knows what else.

The difference between the townsman and the countryman is more widely known than it used to be, because the great facility and speed of modern transport, which has filled the highway with motor vehicles which take us from door to door at a speed rivalled by long distance express trains only, and is filling the sky with still faster aeroplanes, has greatly multiplied the number of people who work in the city and sleep in rural bungalows which quickly become suburban. John Gilpin, living over his shop in Cheapside,[10] has to buy an acre in the country and put a house on it before he realizes that roads and paved streets, ready made boundaries marked by area railways and curbstones, water on tap and light in the open air at night are not natural phenomena.* The same facility of transport which makes this possible for him also makes it so easy and economical to get implements of all sorts from the manufacturing towns that it is harder and harder to find anyone in the suburbs who can make anything or repair anything singlehanded. Even things which are still made by hands instead of by machines are made by so many hands that no individual possessing only two can pretend to make more than a fragment of anything. Thus the townsman can live only as a fragment in a jig-saw puzzle, whereas the husbandman can support himself independently and be his own master and slave to nature only, like a beaver.

* Superfluous holograph addition: But his bungalow is soon

Chapter One

As I have used the word revolutionist pretty often here and elsewhere, I had better explain that I am using it in a sense that is modern; and that I do not mean by it a blood-stained man in shirt sleeves and a red cap of liberty, chopping the Princess Lamballe to pieces with an axe,[1] or a woman sitting before a guillotine and interrupting her knitting occasionally to count the heads of aristocrats as they fall into the basket.[2] I mean one who has adopted the study of the history and practice of revolution as a profession. Revolution is both an art and a branch of political science of the first importance; but this conception of it is quite modern. It is barely thirty years since the conception of politics as a science to be professionally studied received official sanction by the establishment of the London School of Economics and Political Science, which presently became part of the London University.[3] At about the same time, the young Leon Trotsky, son of a prosperous bourgeois farmer or kulak, finished his schooling and had to choose a profession. He had distinguished himself in his mathematical studies and had all the professions to choose from, with special qualifications for physics or engineering. He quite deliberately chose the profession of revolutionist, and became not only a professor of the history and science of revolution, but a practitioner of its art. He lived by organizing and lecturing to revolutionary groups and by writing for revolutionary papers. It was a very precarious way of living, and, as governments do not tolerate revolutionary activities, an underground one, with frequent flights from the police, aliases, disguises, and occasional spells of prison and exile. To a man in Trotsky's social position it was made eligible as a career only by a burning religious zeal and irresistible vocation which made all its perils and privations seem worth while. Still, it was in every sense a profession and a learned one.

Trotsky was not the first professional revolutionist, nor even one of the first generation of them. Karl Marx and Friederich [*sic*] Engels in England and Ferdinand Lassalle [4] in Germany were the first notable revolutionists who claimed to be scientific. Marx and Lassalle, sprung from well-to-do Jewish families, were expensively schooled, and, when they became revolutionary socialists, insisted that Socialism had become scientific, and, as Lassalle put it, was taking the field equipped with all the culture of the age. Prince Peter Kropotkin,[5] a Russian revolutionist, was a man of science, and treated all political subjects accordingly. They created a whole generation of "scientific Socialists", including the English Fabians, of whom I was one; [6] but the Fabians did not adopt Socialism as a means of livelihood. Trotsky's generation may be numbered as the third from Marx; and not only he but Lenin and several of his contemporaries did begin their adult life by formally deciding to be revolutionists by profession exactly as they might have decided to be clergymen, or White Fathers,[7] or chemists or astronomers.

To young men with a contempt for riches and personal
luxury, [and with] sufficient courage to live dangerously, it
was an attractive profession.

The significance of this is that when the existing order
broke up catastrophically in Russia it found, what no political movement, revolutionary or constitutional, had enjoyed
since the reforms of Stein and Hardenberg [8] in [hiatus in
MS.], the triumph of Free Trade and Laissez-faire in England,[9] and the revolution made by the Elder Statesmen in
Japan in 1867: [10] that is, leaders who had been specifically
and scientifically educated for their job.

The contrast between them and their enemies the ruling
Cabinet ministers of the Capitalist States was very marked.
The Cabinets were manned by unashamed amateurs and
ignoramuses who had never heard of political science and
were experts only in electioneering and party organization
and intrigue. They never shewed the slightest consciousness
of the writings of the long line of economists and sociologists
from Turgot to Cobden and Bright who had built up the
theory of the capitalist system.[11] They drifted along cheer-
fully, taking the line of least resistance to property, privilege,
and aristocracy, and of greatest resistance to the proletariat,
just as things turned up. At one moment they would be fulfilling the Cromwellian law (as important as Newton's laws
of motion) that no man goes farther than the man who does
not know whither he is going; and at the next they would
sink to the level of a preparatory school for the sons of
gentlemen desiring a seat in parliament in addition to the
Oxford or Cambridge hall mark for their male offspring.

But they had one tremendous advantage over the professional revolutionists. Their political technique, such as it
was, was not academic: it was practical and was backed by
an executive civil service with a routine which had been

evolved ad hoc. In parliamentary committees there is con-
stant criticism of Bills by members who are accustomed
to handle large sums of money and deal with bodies of
workers. Cabinets may do everything from the most reactionary point of view, and spend weeks of heated debate
over sectarian documents towards which a Russian revolutionist would feel exactly as the Archbishop of Canterbury
may be presumed to feel towards Joseph Smith's Book of
Mormon [12] or the prophecies of Joanna Southcote; [13] but all
the time they are either doing something or (much more
frequently) preventing something being done, being in contact in either case with facts and people, and not theorizing.
Even when they are vigorously prosecuting the Class War,
as they mostly are, they are indignantly innocent of any
views about it. They have their feet on the ground all the
time; and although they have a set of creeds and principles
which form a complete collection of superstitions from the
dawn of history to a hundred and fifty years ago or there-
abouts, they are so far from connecting them with their political conduct that they will without the smallest sense of
inconsistency order the rites of Mars and Satan to be celebrated in the Christian temples of peace and goodwill towards men, and attend the services with perfect emotional
integrity.

The nineteenth century revolutionists lacked this practical
training. They had a highly rationalized religion, and not
only believed in it, but, having mastered its logic, thought
they knew why they believed in it. This gave them intellectual power and personal resolution and devotion. They
also had an underground technique of propaganda and
police evasion. They knew all the shifts of poverty, and had
no illusions about the pomps and vanities of Capitalist rule
and pseudo-Christianity. They were accustomed to work on

equal terms with women; and gave no quarter to Capitalist morality and immorality as substitutes for right and wrong, of which they had an abnormally cultivated sense. When some sensitive and religious little woman like Spiridonova, confronted with some deputy autocrat who was abusing his powers beyond all bearing, summarily shot him and took the revolting consequences in the way of savage personal violence, she was to them not a murderess and not a mad-woman: she was a heroine and a martyr. On the moral and intellectual plane they were ultra-realistic; but on the ground of governmental practice and technique, and the financing thereof, they were novices. And their social contacts being necessarily mainly with one another produced a certain in-nocence as to normal human society. Karl Marx unmasked to the world the real condition and relations of the prole-tariat and the bourgeoisie in an epoch making book which it is nevertheless possible to read without believing that Marx had ever spoken to a typical workman or employer in his life. The reading room of the British Museum and the Maitland Park villa,[14] between which Marx spent his very bookish existence, were not resorted to by such company; and the resultant combination of a profound understanding of the historical development and inevitable destiny of the two classes with an almost infantile inexperience of them made the Marxists great in strategy and disastrously ridicu-lous in tactics until its mistakes were hammered out of it by the ruthless discipline of trial and error. Marx never came under that discipline. He knew only that small and un-representative section of the working class which goes to lectures instead of backing horses, and the equally unrepre-sentative members of the middle class and aristocracy who were in revolt against their order, and were sympathisers if not active fellow-conspirators. With the civil and military services which have to tackle the real work of administration behind their puppets in parliament he had no contacts.

This ignorance of the Marxists not only made the bourgeois statesmen of the ruling class uppishly contemptuous of them as unpractical and mischievous visionaries but delivered them into the hands of the police whenever they made their ludicrously inept attempts to put their theory of Class War into practice. But the contempt of the bourgeois for the Marxist was shallow and feeble compared with the contempt and hatred of the Marxist for the bourgeois. For the Marxist ignorance of practical administration was balanced by the ignorance of the optimistically educated and personally comfortable ruling class as to the fearful mass of individual human suffering and degeneration wrought by Capital in pursuit of profits and rents (lumped as Surplus Value by Marx); and of this the Marxists, even the well-to-do ones, had an almost maddening knowledge. It gave them a new scale of moral values which reduced the bourgeois scale to the discipline imposed by self-preservation on gangsters and pirates. Thus the sense of intellectual superiority derived by the Marxist from his equipment of conscious and hard studied political science and historical theory was reinforced by a sense of ethical superiority which made moral relations between bourgeois and Marxist almost impossible. An insuperable reciprocal arrogance stood between them; and even now, when the Marxists have been humbled and disillusioned on the practical side by their conquest of power in Russia, and the bourgeois is struggling for life in the financial quicksand into which his Capitalist lights have misled him, the Marxist looks down from his pinnacle of civilization on the bourgeois as a heathen savage, whilst the

bourgeois sees in the Marxist only a criminal on whom he
would set the police if he dared, and will if he ever feels
strong enough.

Obviously the Marxist's is still the greater arrogance.
When he was an underground conspirator it was worse. The
revolutionist was nearly always poor: he was often a Jew;
and as an enemy of Capitalist society he was usually known
to and wanted by the police. It is inconceivable by a well-
to-do law-abiding, churchgoing member of the governing
class that such a disreputable person could look down on
him with an absolutely convinced contempt. Envy of his
riches, jealousy of his eminence, resentful ignorance of the
necessity for a class structure of society, and the bad influence of "professional agitators" on the half educated: all
this he is prepared for amd [sic] ready to deal with by the
strong hand. But that an ignominious and penniless undesirable should regard him as a savant regards an ignoramus, as
a village doctor regards the village idiot, as a magistrate regards a thief, as an aristocrat regards a tradesman: this is
inconceivable to him except as the delusion of a madman.
A treaty between them is impossible. If A considers himself
a first rate person and B a tenth rate person, and B has precisely the same relative estimate of himself and A, then A
and B will never agree; and if one falls into the hands of the
other he will be mishandled. The pride of race, antiquity,
and divine favor, which makes every Jew despise every
Gentile; the pride of nationality which makes the Irishman
despise everyone on earth who is not Irish; and all the other
prides, great and small, which prop up the rickety self-
respect of poor humanity in a world of humiliations, are as
nothing compared to the pride of the Marxist who holds the
keys of history, past and future, in his hands, and sees our
great Capitalist Kingdoms and Churches and parliaments

and powers as tawdry pageants whose banners have a filthily seamy side turned away from the public, and sees the actors, for all their airs of leading and ordering the world, as the merest flies on the wheel of an evolutionary process which not one of them understands.

There was an element of hero worship, even of theocracy in this. The revolutionists, having almost all flung the gods of the Churches out of their minds, left a vacuum which, abhorred by nature, was immediately filled by the sage of Haverstock Hill. Marx was set up as an omniscient and infallible philosophic historian, economist, and prophet. Now Marx was like other mortal geniuses, right in the lump, but occasionally wrong in the little. It seemed impossible that Stanley Jevons, who, after sowing his intellectual wild oats in Australia, was no sooner settled in a university chair at home than he proceeded to stem the flowing tide of Socialism by demonstrating the impracticability of a State parcel post, could have thought out a sound theory of value when Marx, by a fairly obvious oversight, had thought out a wrong one; but it was so. As to the materialist theory of history, even so fanatical an English Marxist as Henry Mayers Hyndman pointed out that it was knocked into a cocked hat by the history of Peru.[15] Marx's mistakes did not matter to Socialism, just as the mistakes of Adam Smith (who was similarly wrong in his theory of value) did not matter to Free Trade; for they were not really fundamental, and were indeed very unnecessary and pretentious complications of very simple situations. His big category of surplus value was none the less real because he failed to analyse it and account for it correctly, and could consequently be shewn to be in the wrong by comparatively trumpery official economists who were not, in the large, worthy to lace his boots. But the Marxists would insist on his infallibility. To this day it is dangerous to make fun of Marx worship in Russia as Mr H. G. Wells did.[16] And it is in fact not wise for a Russian to do so, because so many people are color-blind to everything that is not either as black as soot or as white as snow, that when I was converted by Philip Wicksteed to the Jevonian value theory,[17] I was immediately accused by the Marxists of holding that Marx was an imbecile liar and impostor, and that * Socialism was a delusion and a fraud, thereby reminding me of a sceptical colonel of my acquaintance who held that the inspiration of the Bible had been conclusively disproved by the fact that the rector's housemaid had brought forth an illegitimate child of which the rector's own son was the father.

However, as Islam is none the less a great world fact because Mahomet thought that the mountains were great weights placed on the world by Allah to prevent its being blown away, and made a disastrously wrong calendar,[18] Communism will not be baulked of its destiny by Marx's few slips. And it was the contempt for all non-Marxists—for the infidel, in fact—with which he inspired his disciples that nerved them to turn the Russian world upside down as they did when their moment came. The extreme Conservatives and the Marxists have one tremendous force in common. They both know that they are right and that their opponents are wrong. They are Diehards, and, when it comes to the final issue, will kill and stand to be killed.

But all revolutionists are not Marxists. The Marxists are highly educated intellectuals, and therefore in a minority in the underground movement which gathers to itself everyone who has a grudge against society. It is a mistake to suppose that it gathers criminals; for criminals are mostly as conventional in their views as any respectable bourgeois.

* MS. has] thet

The common thief has the most complete respect for property and belief in it as an institution, and is as certain as the prison chaplain that he is doing wrong. Proudhon's proposition that property is theft,[19] a truism to the Socialist, would not strike a common thief even as a paradox: he would dismiss * it as a monstrous lie, and refuse to believe that any sane man ever said or thought such a thing. In a riot or insurrection he may join the rioters or rebels on the chance of looting; but as to joining an underground conspiracy which offers him all the risks of the criminal, from police persecution to the perils of a missionary among cannibals, with absolutely no asset except the approval of his conscience, he would regard that as a mug's game, and an incomprehensibly silly one at that. A convinced Socialist may be a rascal just as a burglar may be a convinced Baptist; but in neither case is he living up to his principles: on the contrary, he is disgracefully false to them.

Nevertheless revolutionists in their underground phase— and when they come uppermost they † are no longer revolutionists—are a very mixed lot. Their solidarity is an illusion: their quarrels are notorious. Marx quarrelled with everybody who did not echo him and with some people who did: with Proudhon, whose Philosophy of Poverty he called the Poverty of Philosophy; with Bakunin; with Hyndman: [20] all of them out-and-out revolutionists like himself. And this was not always mere cantankerousness or jealousy of leadership: there were genuine differences of doctrine and policy to quarrel about. The movement necessarily recruited malcontents of every description, from Nationalists and Freethinkers who would join any movement that was anti-imperialist and anti-clerical to fanatical doctrinaires of the most complicated and fantastic Utopianism. One rough but

* MS. has: dismoss   † MS. has: thay

real diamond in the English movement, who went to prison repeatedly for his faith, Jack Williams, was first led to question the justice of the capitalist system by his naïve belief that Orton the Tichborne Claimant,[21] who was sentenced to penal servitude after an interminable trial for pretending to be Sir Roger Tichborne, was a laboring man who had been done out of his rights. At the conclusion of one of my own propagandist lectures a workman came to me and assured me of his entire agreement with everything I had said. "But," he added, "it is all no use; for the only man who could have set us to rights is dead." I asked who this gifted individual might be. He at once named Orton's famous Counsel, Dr Kenealy, who had been disbarred for calling witnesses in whose good faith, it was held, he could not possibly have believed. Besides these simple souls, who, like Williams, soon got educated by the Socialists, there were republicans, currency cranks, general-strikemongers, single-taxers, humanitarians, fifth-monarchists, and all sorts of eccentrics with all sorts of bees in their bonnets, besides the steady and reputable "advanced" Liberals, Tory Democrats, Anglo-Catholics, Quakers, and charitable social workers. Most of these people were bound to drop off if Marxism really came to business; for they were malcontents and reformers with no comprehension of either Communism or Capitalism as complete and incompatible systems of society. Only a negligible percentage of them had read Marx.

But there were certain main divisions who were certain to sunder the ranks of even the genuine revolutionists, who were all agreed that the proletariat must realize its position ("become class-conscious" was the catchword) and expropriate the proprietariat before a stable and honest society could be achieved. These were the anarchists, the syndicalists, the social-democrats, and the Marxist Communists.

Of these the most troublesome and the most English were
the anarchists, who were libertarians and individualists first,
and Socialists a long and reluctant way after. Some of them
called themselves anti-State Communists or Communist-
Anarchists, insisting on a condition of freedom in which
there should be as far as possible no State, no officials, no
compulsions, and even no institutions. They were so innocent of the arts of government and so unconscious of the
part it played in their own lives that they thought these
negations quite possible. They were also ignorant of the
pons asinorum of political economy: the law of rent,[22] which
in any individualist system must inevitably produce a plutocracy, and, at a certain pressure of population, a proletariat. They saw plainly enough that government is at present an organization of slavery; and having a constitutional
objection to slavery they thought that if we could get rid of
government we should get rid of slavery. But in truth such
a riddance would only complicate slavery with brigandage;
for the slavery that governments must organize in order to
minimize it, is not of their making: it is the slavery to Nature, which ordains ruthlessly that we must produce our *
subsistence by our labor or perish, and that as the most essential things are the most perishable we must live not by
hoarding but from hand to mouth, each year living on its
own harvest, and can by no means really perform the five
per cent miracle believed in by bankers and stockbrokers, of
consuming twenty years future harvests in one year, or de-
ferring consumption of the present harvest for twenty
years.†

We now see that a successful revolution must leave a
multitude of its makers and supporters tragically disap-

* MS. has: out
† Longhand note—not in Shaw's hand: This ends the shorthand
sent from S. Africa

pointed. We write glibly that those who make half revolutions dig their own graves; but their risk is not so great as that of those who make whole revolutions. The moment a revolution becomes a government it necessarily sets to work to exterminate revolutionists. Quite the most ridiculous exhibition I saw in Soviet Russia was the revolutionary museum in Moscow, devoted to the glorification of the heroes and martyrs who suffered and often perished in the struggle between Socialism and Capitalist Imperialism that lasted for seventy years before the triumph of the proletariat in Russia in 1917, and that is still going on throughout the rest of the world. Many of them had been personally known to me. Most of them, in their frock coats and long beards, seemed strangely and solemnly respectable, and, compared with Russian commissars, enormously futile. They had talked and written and got themselves into trouble and been beaten every time by the bourgeois police. The women, more practical, had killed a petty tyrant or two who had gone too far. Spiridinova, for instance. I forget the name of the intolerable scoundrel she shot when it became quite plain that his death was as necessary as that of a cobra let loose in a nursery, and no man would take on the job. She was beaten to a jelly for it and otherwise horribly maltreated: I suppose because killing her would have been too merciful.[23] But what a woman! A gentle, slight, delicate and devoted district visitor, dressed as for a British rectory breakfast on Sunday morning. What must she, who lived to become the heroine of the revolution, have thought of its ruthless suppression of revolutionists? We know what Kropotkin, the gentle, the noble, the Christ-like Kropotkin (how he would have repudiated the comparison!) felt about it? [sic] I know what Tolstoy's daughter felt about it: she told me herself; for she had seen a smiling countryside where good farming had brought to everybody such prosperity as was possible for them in the days of Tsardom, blasted into ruin and desolation, squalor and misery, by the Soviet expropriation and persecution of the Kulak. I visited Krupskaya, Lenin's widow, the most fascinating widow in the world, a woman to be adored by children and courted by savants; and the story went that she had given the Soviet a piece of her mind so roundly that Stalin had threatened that if she did it again he would appoint another widow for Lenin. Gorki, too, the sensitive, the hater of cruelty and injustice, the discoverer of touching virtues in the most impossible people: to him the revolution has not brought the millennium, though he can forgive it as he can forgive worse things.

I do not reproach the Soviet Government for not making these angels of the revolution perfectly happy: they would be unhappy in the Garden of Eden because the cats played cruelly with the mice before devouring them. Much less do I reproach it for frankly shooting anarchists and syndicalists who in the old unkind days were their comrades and helpers and fellow sufferers, or for handling Socialists who are also advocates of western parliamentary methods as more dangerous to the dictatorship of the proletariat than a British Conservative Prime Minister (even an ex-Socialist one). But I certainly laughed at the Soviet for setting up a museum in Moscow to glorify revolution. For when the revolution triumphs revolution becomes counter-revolution. The young Russian fired with enthusiasm for the glorious old slayers of Tsars, Grand Dukes, and chiefs of police, and finding this species of game as extinct as the buffalo, may try his hand on Stalin, on the commissars, and on the chiefs of the G.P.U. There are always grievances enough to excite our Charlotte Cordays, who will do and suffer anything for a halo.

Those museums need drastic overhauling. Their object

should be, not to idolize revolutionists as such, but rather to excuse them and to train future sufferers from the Tolstoyan World Betterment Craze [24] (*Weltverbesserungswahn*) not to attack Governments *qua* Governments, and not to be disappointed and driven into reaction when they find that even after the most millennial revolution there are still unmanageable people to make coercive work for the new police. Also that the exasperating people who declare that all the problems of government will yield to Love must be suppressed under any conceivable government as invincibly ignorant of the existence of any such problems.

One of the first tasks facing a Government is to lay down the conditions on which it can afford to grant life and liberty to persons within its jurisdiction. That such liberty is an unlimited and unconditional natural right is absurd: if a government conceded the right to live to a mad dog, the people would take the law into their own hands and kill it, probably with unnecessary cruelty. Every real Government must assume powers of life and death. And every civilized government must reserve that right for itself, and strictly suppress duelling and private murder in all its forms. And this immediately brings it up against two sorts of people: those who want to carry arms and settle their quarrels for themselves by simply fighting them out, and those who have such a horror of killing that they cannot endure the idea of its being sanctioned and practised officially. Thousands of people will sign a petition for the reprieve of a murderer, and, when their petition is successful, and the sentence is changed from sudden death to the slow death of imprisonment for life, will at once be perfectly satisfied and forget all about him. They will not take part in an American lynching; but if the delinquent is thrust out of the city to wander in the sage brush and perish in agomies [agonies] of thirst they are quite satisfied. Clearly this is not a humanitarian instinct: it must be an atavistic dread of the blood feud or of having to pay blood money to a slain person's kindred. It needs a strong handed Government to put down the duellists, and a strongheaded one to override the so-called sentimentalists.

The Soviet deals with the difficulty in a very sensible and Christian manner. It has abolished capital punishment. Any reasonable and not too cruel sort of murder to which a normally selfcontrolled person can be provoked can be settled by four years of an imprisonment which, to a "poor white" in a capitalistic country, would seem a privilege to be earned rather than a penalty to be dreaded. But the criminal law is quite a distinct matter from the very necessary process politely paraphrased as weeding the garden.[25] Most of the deliberate killing done in this world is utilitarian killing which no sane person dreams of associating with crime and punishment, innocence and guilt, expiation and sacrifice. We kill animals for food on an enormous scale. We kill rabbits and stags to keep down the rabbit and stag population, which would otherwise eat us out of house and home. We kill cancer patients with morphia to put them out of their misery. We kill unborn infants lest they should kill their mothers later on. We sacrifice and kill soldiers by the million under various pretexts, mostly hypocritical or nonsensical. When we can find no pretext for war we kill for sport. We remove these killings from the category of murder. It is inevitable that weeding the garden should be at least equally privileged, with, of course, the weeds vehemently dissenting.

I believe that very few of the compassionate people who become revolutionists because they cannot endure the cruelties and injustices of "capital in pursuit of surplus value" ever realize that if the supreme political power came into their hands, one of the first things they would have to do would be to sign somebody's death warrant, and that a dogmatic refusal to do so would only lead to some crueller way of weeding the garden. When the success of a revolution, far from immediately reducing the number of executions and emptying the prisons, has for the moment a horrifyingly contrary effect, they turn against the revolution, and produce the familiar phenomenon of the most amiable of the revolutionists becoming the bitterest of reactionaries. The Russian revolution has suffered more than any previous one from this sort of reaction because it is a revolution in morals as well as in the form of government. Our English changes from prelacy to presbyterianism, from a hereditary monarch to a rebel Lord Protector,[26] and from both to an oligarchy and an established episcopal Church which presently dethroned the native Catholic king and replaced him by a foreign Protestant one, did not alter our customary interpretation of the ten commandments. The crimes for which men were still hanged, drawn, quartered, and beheaded were the same old crimes for which people were accustomed to see them beheaded. There were terrors and proscriptions in which the top dogs of the moment tried to exterminate the bottom dogs; but they did it on the same old pretexts. This was true also of the revolution in America. Washington, like Cromwell, was considered shockingly disloyal and no gentleman; but both stood equally for liberty, which was one of the ideals of the crowd, and for the conventional interpretation of the ten commandments.

The French revolution went a little deeper. In its moment of extreme danger from its emigrant nobles and their fellow nobles throughout Europe it made aristocracy a capital crime; and some of the commissioners whom it entrusted with the executions were drunken blackguards who became homicidal lunatics when their heads were turned with power. But they were all steeped in sentimental morality of a quite popular kind. Robespierre was a champion prig whose last reproach to his opponents before they killed him was to call them assassins. Marat was driven crazy by his entirely conventional and charitable pity for the sufferings of the poor which he had witnessed as a medical general practitioner.[27] The revolution was savagely anti-proletarian and bigotedly bourgeois: it was far safer to be a marquis in Paris under Robespierre than to be a Socialist, as Cadoudal[28] found to his cost. The ordinary man of business had everything to gain and nothing to lose by the success of the revolution economically; and morally his habitual assumptions were not only unchallenged but boosted to the then fashionable level of ancient Roman virtue.

Compared to the French revolution the revolutions of 1832 and 1848 were trumpery affairs, quite moral conventionally. The moral challenge of the Paris commune of 1871 was instantly and ferociously stamped out, and too little understood by the shallow snobbery of its exterminators to be seriously discussed by them.

1917 was a very different matter. All the previous revolutions had accepted the middle class tradition of respectability. They respected the respectable, supported the respectable, and left them respectable. Let me make the situation more vivid by availing myself of John Galsworthy's invaluable contribution to modern sociology called the Forsyte Saga. The Forsytes, with one foot in the city and the other in the country, half squirarchs, half—I had almost written plutarchs, but out of respect for a famous ancient biographer must write plutocrats—they enjoyed a position almost sacred in general esteem as well as in their own. There is a great deal to be said for them as a class. They produced Mr Galsworthy, virtuous enough to loathe them. They produced me, at an impoverished remove or two, also virtuous enough to loathe them. The statistics of Galton [29] give a scientific backing to the prejudice of Dean Inge in their favour as, on the whole, our solidest and ablest class. They have their social equivalents all over civilized Europe and America, though we in England believe that the English variety is—if I may combine the language of Scripture with that of the Stock Exchange—the head of the corner.

The Soviet shoots them at sight.

I will not attempt to extenuate this enormity; but I admit, in justice to the Soviet, that it is the only thing to be done with forsytes in a society aiming at permanence and gifted with an economic conscience. For the forsyte, with all his virtues, is an incorrigible and unashamed thief. In all the countries in which he holds the political power he has made laws to allow and enforce the particular methods of thieving practised by him, and founded institutions and ceremonies and titles to dignify them. But when he finds himself in a country where he has no such power and has therefore made no such laws, he inevitably falls into the hands of the police, who, on discovering after due examination that he is not a common delinquent who knows that he is doing wrong, and is apologetically willing to make reasonably credible professions of regret and promises of amendment, but is actually proud of his exploits, parades his booty, and claims high respect and privilege on the strength of it, besides bringing up his children to walk in his ways, conclude that there is nothing to be done but weed the garden. There is something half tragic, half comic, and wholly pitiable in the spectacle of Soames Forsyte falling into the hands of a communist gamekeeper and being liquidated as vermin; yet such events are inevitable and irremediable under the stern morality of Communism, with its fundamental tenet that whoever does not by his own personal service produce during his lifetime enough to repay the advances made to him in bringing him up and educating him, to replace what he consumes in his prime, and to provide for his superannuation, with a surplus to give to the national capital fund, inflicts on the community precisely the same injury as a thief, and must, if his example spreads, bring his country to ruin. There is no getting away from this fundamental fact. Soames can only plead that if you kill him you rob his fellow-countrymen of their incentive to become forsytes, to which the Russian reply is "Precisely. Bang!"

There is no way of becoming rich in Russia because there is no way of becoming poor, the two words having no meaning except reciprocally. If you want to have more bread than other people can get if they want it, then—Bang! If you are an inventor or discoverer you will be received with open arms; but if you demand a patent, so that the fruits of your discovery will be appropriated by you and your family alone and all the rest will have to go on working as hard as if your discovery had never been made—Bang! Do not mistake the Russian attitude: the Soviet does not shoot you out of insane hostility to invention and discovery. It shoots you simply because you are no gentleman. Or, to put it positively, because you are a bourgeois or forsyte. And who can deny that this is a very sufficient reason? Within the memory * of my grandfather the bourgeoisie hanged small children in rows for petty thefts from the rich. Need he now be surprised at finding himself added to the festoon for colossal thefts from the poor?

Compare this shooting plan with ours. We do not let Soames off scot free. We let him rob the poor and then rob

* MS. has: momory

him and scatter the money to the unemployed to prevent their being driven by actual starvation to liquidate Soames and burn his house on their own account in their fury. In this we are half-revolutionists digging our own graves. We are stealing from Socialism the distributive half of it that can be practised without thought by our lazy goodnature and our generosity with other people's money, omitting the difficult and stern productive and constructive half on which all the rest depends. Anything more resourceless, more feebleminded, more utterly void of what Englishmen * boast of as "character" could not be imagined. When we have heaped surtax and death duties on Soames until his property, the means by which he steals and lives, is wrested from him without any sort of compensation in three generations or less, and he himself falls into the ranks of the unemployed, we cannot even find him a job: we can only stop his mouth with the plunder of the newly rich Soameses who are not yet stripped naked. Unless one of these will give him a job he must take the dole, a quarter of which will be promptly taken away from him as rent by the particular Soames who owns the few feet of English earth on which he sleeps, and must loaf miserably about the streets until for want of anything better to do he joins a string of his companions in misfortune who are passing the time by marching with a banner inscribed "We want work, not charity," and, after listening to a few speeches from Communist agitators who tell him how much better they manage in Russia, has his head broken by the police. In Russia they would regard his head as a valuable object and find a use for it. For in Russia they have a really responsible government, a government which accepts the fundamental responsibility of all civilized governments, the responsibility for organising the

* MS. has: Englishment

work by which its citizens must live, and taking care that nobody shall live by shirking his or her share of it.

If our forsytes were reasonably happy people as well as materially comfortable people I should perhaps feel more compassionately about the Russian plan of exterminating them. But my observation of them convinces me that they have a very poor time of it, and that they would have a worse if they had not partly invented for themselves, and partly had shoved on to them by their commercial parasites, a routine of travelling, sport, dress, idolatrous court cere-monial and Church ritual, which is as compulsory on them as real work is in Russia and much more expensive and ex-hausting. To escape from it the brainy ones and the handy ones take up political or professional or agricultural or finan-cial work, thereby putting themselves in the position of the Irishman in the bottomless sedan chair who said "But for the honor and glory of it I might as well have walked". No-body will persuade me that a Russian surveyor or town planner has not a better time of it than a British forsyte on the golf links, meanly rejoicing in his opponent[']s muffs and mishaps, and looking back to nothing more useful than having done the fourteenth hole in two. As a convinced Communist I strive to rescue the rich from their riches with much more personal tenderness than to rescue the poor from their poverty; for the most miserable state pos-sible to Man is to feel wasted; and the rich are going to waste all over the place, whilst the poor, though their time also is wasted to an enormous degree in disabling the rich by taking their natural healthy work out of their hands and preying on them, have at least some pride in being serviceable.

After all, a forsyte, if he has sense to see that the forsyte game is up, and makes up his mind to Communism, can get

on well enough in Russia at the cost of a white lie—or
should I say a Red lie? All that he has to do is to claim that
his father was a peasant who worked on the land with his
hands. His own hands, like Lenin's, may convince anybody
at the first glance that nobody in his family has done manual
work since the Conquest (or its Russian equivalent); but no
matter: men with the forsyte literacy and habit of ordering
other people about are wanted in Russia until the emancipated proletarians have grown their own stock (a process already well advanced); and it is easy to deceive the Soviet
when it wishes to be deceived.

The persecution of the intelligentsia in Russia did not last
very long. It was, I think, justified at the time when it was
not yet perceived to be impracticable. I have often said myself that if I were a revolutionary dictator my first care
would be to see that persons with a university education, or
with the acquired mentality which universities inculcate
and stereotype, should be ruthlessly excluded from all direc-
tion of affairs, all contact with education especially with
their own children, and, if not violently exterminated, at
least encouraged to die out as soon as possible. Lenin shared
my views and attempted to carry them into action. If
Napoleon was able to find the very competent generals
whom he made famous as his Marshals in the French stable
yards and attorneys' * offices, and snap his fingers at his
former aristocratic comrades,[30] why should not Lenin do
likewise? But it was no use. Under the Soviet men with the
morals of Napoleon's marshals would have been liquidated
in a week. Trotsky's new army, like Cromwell's New Model,
needed 30,000 officers. The new communal industries re-
quired countless bosses; for Communism does not alter the
natural division of modern mankind into 95 per cent who

* MS. has] attorney's

have their work cut out for them and 5 per cent who can cut it out. The proletarian supply ran short: the bourgeois supply was indispensable. The notice "no bourgeois need apply" was not formally taken down, nor was the ban lifted from the persecuted intelligentsia; but a new classification called The Intellectual Proletariat was set up; and under this heading I was received, when I stepped out of the train at Moscow, by a body of authors, artists, men of science, industrial managers and the like who, with a little Savil[l]e Row or Conduit Street tailoring and here and there a touch of shaving cream, would have been at home in any of our West end [sic] bourgeois clubs. I have no doubt that had I asked them what their fathers were they would all have assured me that the old men were peasants who worked on the land with their hands; but as I should not have believed them I thought it better not to be too inquisitive. After all, it cannot be concealed that Trotsky and Lenin were forsytes by class. Stalin claims to be the grandson of a cobbler; [31] but he was educated for the priesthood, and would pass with any western for a romantically dark eyed Georgian chieftain, or possibly the necessarily illegitimate son of an aristocratic cardinal. I scented the soldier and the ecclesiastic, certainly not the cobbler.

Anyhow, it was plain to me that professional men and women have a better time of it in Russia than in England. As far as I could make out none of them had more than £500 a year and a two room flat to escape overcrowding in, nor any hope of greater luxury for many years to come. This may seem miserable poverty when you have forsytic ideas and standards, and are in commercial competition, and your wife and daughter in social competition, with people ranging from "poor devils with only ten thousand a year" to well-off people with ten thousand a month. It is not agree-

able to have to yield precedence to the peerage, the commissioned ranks of the army, and the Foreign Office, and
to be regarded by them as an Untouchable. If your tastes
and needs are simple, it is exasperating to have to spend a
thousand a year on appearances of one sort or another before you can call a penny that you earn really your own, and
to have rents and prices generally forced up against you
by the careless expenditure of rich forsytes who explain to
you that the secret of comfortable travelling (and staying at
home) is to "never mind what it costs". You can hardly go
into good society and hold your own there and get your
daughters well married without at least five or six thousand
a year net unless you are a duke impoverished by death
duties or a king in exile. In Russia all this has passed away
like an evil dream. Any of it that made any serious difficulty
about passing away has been shot away. You are not poor
with five hundred a year because nobody is richer than
you. You are esteemed for your professional competence
and for nothing else. When you are not busy on your job,
you can do what you like, go where you like, wear what you
like, marry whom you like (if he or she will), get fair play
in the courts and consideration from the authorities, and
be free from anxiety as to the future of your wife and children to an extent unknown and incredible in Forsyte society.

Now the maintenance of this earthly paradise for professional men (for such it must appear to our struggling,
anxious, impecunious doctors, parsons, authors, artists, inventors, scholars, briefless barristers and minor solicitors)
is really based, finally and fundamentally, on the new institution of forsyte shooting, which takes the place of pheas-
ant shooting in England except that it is always in season.
It is not done quite as thoroughly as one could desire, be-

cause, as Lenin soon found, it is necessary to leave to private trade all the ground in Russia that has not yet been covered by communism, and private trade is a hotbed of Forsytism; but there is enough of it to remind all Russians of their obligations to the community to pay their way like ladies and gentlemen, with something over to make the world better for their posterity; and the Soviet loses no opportunity of making the lot of the forsytic private trader less eligible than that of the communist financially, even without reckoning his knowledge that the moment the communist organisation is ready to take over his business it will do so as ruthlessly and with as little consideration for his vested interests than [sic] our big multiple shops shew when they extinguish petty single-trade shops by the dozen.

This forsyte shooting then is the specific feature of the Russian revolution which scandalizes those who have long ago ceased to regard the French and American revolutions less favorably than the compulsion of King John by his barons to sign Magna Charta. This is not accounted for wholly by the lapse of time. We have had a brand new revolution in Spain, in which the king had to run for his life and very nearly lost it. We made no more fuss about that than if it had been an oldfashioned No Popery riot [32] or the plundering of the Church by Henry VIII.[33] But this shooting of gentlemen on the ground that they are no gentlemen, this excommunication of the direct selfhelp which has been the ideal of our respectable middl[e] classes from Defoe to Samuel Smiles,[34] this attack on that highest aspiration of British humanity, the attainment to "independent means" as high treason, this treatment of benefactors who give half crown tips to railway porters and hundred guinea tips to hospitals as mad dogs or mosquitoes: all this is beyond any-

thing that even Tennyson, in his sense of British superiority
to "the mad fool fury of the Seine",[35] could have believed
possible.

But there can be [no] question that it is good business. I
should be sorry to take a pistol in my own hand and blow
off the back of poor old Soames's pate, just as Soames himself would be sorry to operate similarly on Stalin; but I
cannot conceal from myself that the thing has got to be done
if our civilization is not to go the way of all the previous
civilisations [sic] which have been forsyted into bankruptcy
and bygoneness. If Soames, damn him, would be content
to be a thief, boldly carrying into business the stirring traditions of a robber aristocracy, I might be disposed to let
him off with a pretty stiff surtax on his plunder. But the
fellow will have it that he is an honorable man; that he is
the source of all the empire's wealth and greatness; that
he has invented all the machinery and devised all the social
organization without which we should still be woadstained
savages; that he is a pillar of religion and a vessel of divine
grace; that without him England would not be what she is
(which is true, by the way, worse luck); that his unsocial
acquisitiveness is national thrift; that his conceited snobbery is self-respect; that his victims are spendthrifts and
drunkards, and his communist opponents scoundrels, anarchists, and atheists: in short, that his parasitic condition
is the model destiny towards which every righteous person
should strive. And as he controls all the newspapers and
has the keys of all the Church of England pulpits and most
of the Free Church ones in his pocket, he actually does
persuade the very people whom he has smoked out of their
hard earnings like bees to supply him with rent and dividends, to accept his monstrous pretensions and to feel that
if he perished England perishes. Well, he has perished in

of our respectable middl. classes from Defoe to Samuel Smiles,this attack on that highest aspiration of British humanity,the attainment to of " independent means" is high treason, this treatment of benefactors who give half crown tips to railway porters and hundred guinea tips to hospitals as mad dogs or mosquitoes: all this is beyond anything that even Tennyson,in his sense of British superiority to "the mad fool fury of the Seine",could have believed possible.

But there can be question that it is good business. I should be sorry to take a pistol in my own hand and blow off the back of poor old Soames's pate, just as himself would be sorry to operate similarly on Stalin; but I cannot conceal from myself that the thing has got to be done if our civilization is not to go the way of all the previous civilisations which have been carried into bankruptcy and bygoneness. boldly carrying into business the stirring traditions of a robber aristocracy, If Soames, damn him, would be content to be a thief,I might be disposed to let him off with a pretty stiff surtax on his plunder. But the fellow will have it that he is an honorable man;that he is the source of all the empire's wealth and greatness;that he has invented all the machinery and devised all the social organization without which we should still be woadstained savages;that he is a killer of religion and a vessel of divine grace; that without him England would not be what she is (which is true,by the way,worse luck);that his unsocial acquisitiveness national thrift;his conceited snobbery,self-respect;his victims,spendthrifts and drunkards,and his communist opponents scoundrels, anarchists, and atheists : in short, that his present conditions the model destiny towards which every righteous person should strive. And as he controls all the newspapers and has the keys of all the Church of England pulpits and most of the free church ones in his pocket,he actually does persuade the very people whom he has smoked out of their

Russia; and Russia is all the better for it, as Sinbad the Sailor was the better for getting the old man of the sea off his back. Yet it is still believed in our suburbs that Sinbad exists only to carry the old man about; and they willingly let him take from them the enormous sums by which he retains an army and navy, a police force and an air force, to keep Sinbad in order in case he should shew any signs of coming to his senses and buck jumping. And so he not only robs us but corrupts our morals, stultifies our intellects, and damns our souls. From the Communist point of view there is no arguing with that sort of thing. There is nothing for it but Bang.

That obvious conclusion is just what we will not admit. I think there is now a very general agreement among those who have any economic outlook that Soames's old nineteenth century excuses—reward of abstinence, custodianship of culture, individual liberty, freedom of speech and Press, and trade, overpopulation, constitutional safeguards against tyranny and the rest of it—are now played out. They never stood disinterested examination as arguments; and the facts are now smashing them without any argument at all. It is now more than fifty years since Cairnes, an honest Emeritus professor of political economy, told the forsytes what they are: drones in the hive.[36] But instead of going on to draw the obvious moral that working men must treat parasitic ones as working bees treat drones, he said sulkily that as we had contracted to maintain them we must go on maintaining. This did not impress me, as I, for one, had never contracted to do anything of the sort. But Cairnes said so; and Soames breathed again. Our ablest contemporary economists are just as clear about the drone part of the business; but as they spring from the forsyte class themselves, they break down over the Russian solution, and drivel about liberty. Now it is precisely Soames's claim to an unnatural liberty to do what he likes all the time instead of producing his own keep, which means that he shoves that duty on to someone else, that makes it necessary to exterminate him as a destroyer of liberty. I must really ask our economists to face the situation and be reasonable about it.

However, let us see whether we could not spare their feelings to some extent. My own position is rather ambiguous: my animal parasitical depredations are quite considerable. I prey on theatres all over the world. I levy tolls on railways I never saw and to whose construction and upkeep I have never contributed a farthing. I plunder the peaceful and refined homesteads of the garden cities and force the miner to toil in the dangerous underground to keep me in luxury after he has provided a few necessities for himself. It would not be strictly accurate to say that for me the Ceylon diver holds his breath and goes all naked to the hungry shark, because I have not, as a matter of fact, invested in the pearl fisheries, and do not know whether the fishing is still done in that crude way. But that I am quite eligible for liquidation on Russian principles there can be no doubt.

It will be remembered by musicians that Wagner's Wotan, though he became convinced that his time was up, and even set to work at his own extinction,[37] did, when it came to the point, put up some fight. At my advanced age I should not greatly mind being shot: indeed, all revolutionary considerations apart, I am not sure that a good case for shooting me might not be made out on the general ground that I have lived quite as long as the community can be reasonably expected to stand, and that I had better not, like so many other old actors, "lag superfluous". I could no doubt say "If you shoot me I shall not write any more plays"; but that might act as an inducement to the firing party. But there is a mawkish hesitation to shoot me which is reflected in an equally mawkish hesitation on my part to be shot. And there are other reasons. My death and expropriation would mean destitution for about a dozen people who have in no way deserved to suffer for my sins. If I am to be shot they should have had notice. My wife, who would of course be shot along with me, stands equally committed. Of course a Communist Government bent on the shooting would say "Do not trouble about that: we shall provide for your dependants.["] But I should question their ability. I should point out that though shooting is always quite simple and practicable, and "stone dead hath no fellow", immediate provision for the huge parasitic section of the proletariat, the working parasites on the parasites, takes much longer than Bang Bang. They cannot be shot: there are too many of them. They might object. I could on these lines make a strong case for my gradual extinction as against my summary execution.

For instance, why should not the limitation that applies to my literary property apply to all my property? Surely if my property in my plays, which I really did create by my personal labor, is to be ruthlessly curtailed twentyfive years after my death, and totally abolished fifty years after it, why should my property in that Brazilian railway to which I contributed nothing be held sacred for ever and ever? I do not greatly mind being shot fifty years after my death. I dont think anybody would. Not even twentyfive. Why not shoot our forsytes twentyfive years after their deaths, when all the old people for whom they have provided are extinct? It would stop the wicked practice of bringing up young people to be forsytes: a crime for which no damna-

tion could be too fiery. When I think of the young people
whose lives I have seen blighted and wasted by their in-
heritance or expectation of independent incomes I can
scarcely contain my wrath. Shooting is far too good for
anyone capable of defending it.

And this brings me to the question of the children in
Russia, and to their education.[38] I saw nothing of the hideous
aftermath of the war: the hordes of deserted or orphaned
child bandits, diseased, derelict, taking refuge at night from
the terrible winter cold in the cooling asphalt containers of
the street menders, following the weather from region to region as the seasons changed, dividing their little common-
wealths spontaneously into scrupulous and timid, into little
children who would not or dare not steal but who would spy
out the land and locate the booty for the bolder and stronger
who did the actual stealing, and, most amazing of all to our
forsytes, their equal division of the spoils between big and
little, bold and cowardly, strong and weak. There were millions of such children in Russia (and elsewhere) after the
war; and they almost drove the Soviets crazy. When White
Europe set on Red Russia until the Red triumph of Trotsky's
New Model put an end to that stupid attempt of all the
king's horses and all the king's men to set Humpty Dumpty
up again, both sides made attempts to retrieve the little
brigands. The Whites, on charitable bourgeois principles,
would carry them into refuges and appoint teachers and
nurses for them, with funds cadged for in the usual forsyte
way. The Reds did the same in their Communist way. Co-
operation was impossible; for the Whites could make no
truce with wicked Bolsheviks, and the Bolsheviks would not
consent to leave any child to have its morals capitalistically
corrupted by the wicked bourgeoisie. As the tide of battle
ebbed and flowed it was a case of *Sauve qui peut* alternately

in the White and Red refuges. When the Reds came the White teachers and nurses bolted and the children ran wild again. When the Whites recovered their ground the Red nurses and teachers did the same. And in both cases there were new slaughterings and helter-skelter flights of parents from the rival wraths, and more children left orphaned, deserted, and derelict. To balance this there was the mortality among the children, which is assumed to have been frightful, though whether it was as great as in our worst slums cannot be taken as proved in view of the numbers still living to testify that they managed to live on the country in the military manner and survive.

I am afraid that on both sides the rescuers often lost patience with the little vagabonds, and disciplined them as savagely as most of our reformatories would have disciplined them: for they were very difficult subjects, and ran away again and again when captured. I was told that when a boy is captured, properly dressed, fed decently, and given a bed to sleep in and a roof to cover him, he invariably shews his appreciation of these bourgeois luxuries by running away next day, and that not until the whole series of operations has been gone through at least five times is there any chance of inducing him to submit to the blessings of civilization. Even when he is finally reclaimed he is so selfreliant and nomadic that he is restless and undependable in stationary jobs, and does best as a navvy, a journalist, a Communist missionary, or something equally adventurous. What happens to the reclaimed girls I could not make out: even in emancipated Russia they retain our habit of thinking they have accounted for everybody when they have accounted for the boys.

But the problem of the wild children is necessarily an ephemeral one. In Moscow and Petersburg (only the tourists

call it Leningrad) they have been completely rounded up:
at least I saw no sign of them there. In the country I saw
the domesticated children of the uncommunized peasant
proprietors; and they certainly were dirty little savages;
but they were living with their parents in the English agricultural fashion. In striking contrast to them were the children on the collective farm, who were so appallingly civilized that my first impulse was to denounce them as a parcel
of insufferable little Marxian prigs. They were much too
clean and well behaved and prettily dressed—as far as they
were dressed at all. When a small and very prettily got up
little girl sang a Sunday school song about how happy and
glorious it was to work for the commune, I pinched myself
to assure myself that I was awake and that this was indeed
Russia and not Canterbury, and this child a genuine little
Bolshevik and not the Dean's youngest daughter. I console
myself with the hope that what I saw was the company
manners of the children dressed up to receive distinguished
visitors, and that the moment our backs were turned they
behaved, as our nurses used to reproach us for behaving,
"like wild Indians", as small children ought to behave.

However, I went to a prison for young delinquents, and
saw there a batch of new arrivals who looked just as unpleasant as a batch of boy criminals in any of our big industrial towns. They were a bad lot, sulky, slouchy, furtively
on their guard against the police or an assault from one of
themselves. They were, I think, all the more suspicious because in Russia "stone walls do not a prisone [sic] make";
and this prison was not a villainous house of torment spotted
all over with half black, half opaque windows like an English jail, but a place rather like Battersea Park, bounded by
split wood pailings [sic] which any moderately enterprising boy could climb over. Several of the lads had just

come in; and the only conclusion they could draw from this absence of such prison arrangements as they could understand was that new, unforeseen, and frightful forms of torture were in store for them. Was not the genial commisar [sic] already beginning to improve their minds as he talked, ostensibly to us, but really over our heads at them. So they slouched at us and stared at us slantwise, and were afraid to pick our pockets lest their unexpected freedom to crowd up to us should be a trap. To get on terms with them we assured them, through the commisar [sic], that though we were persons of the greatest eminence, whose success in life had exceeded the utmost that our most respectable parents could ever have hoped for us, yet the sole reason why we had not fallen into the hands of the police in our youth was that we were not found out. This broke the ice so effectively, and produced such a volley of questions as to what we had done, that we hastily moved on to avoid the dilemma of having either to disappoint them bitterly or else accuse ourselves of all the assassinations and burglaries they were thirsting for.

When we came to the old hands in the workshops we discovered that the cardinal difference between an English and a Russian prison is that in England a delinquent enters as an ordinary man and comes out as a "criminal type", whereas in Russia he enters, like those boys, as a criminal type and would come out an ordinary man but for the difficulty of inducing him to come out at all. As far as I could make out they could stay as long as they liked. In a competitive capitalist State if prisoners are set to do or make anything useful there is a wild clamor from all the private traders that the prisons are taking their business away from them. I can remember when the extensive trade now done in photographs, picture postcards, and all sorts of fine art reproductions at the stalls in our public museums and art galleries, had to be conducted secretly and guiltily lest all the stationers in the neighborhood should terrify the Government with their protests. As to criminals in prisons their right to do anything useful that could possibly be done by a private contractor at a profit is still fiercely contested. But in Russia a prison (if prison it can be called) may be, and indeed is expected to be, as vigorously productive as a farm or factory, and therefore becomes a farm or factory or both. The only sign I saw of anything painful in the place was in the heavy industry shops, where strong lumps of women were operating big machinery whose handling was no child's play, in buildings which had some rather ugly holes and corners. The machines kept them at work intensely; and it may have been their preoccupation with it that gave them a sullen air and gave me a feeling that they objected to be exhibited to bourgeois tourists. Anyhow I cleared out as fast as might be.

Except for this I saw no sign of the way of the transgressor being made unnecessarily hard; and none of these women would have been any better off as innocent persons earning their livings in an English factory. As for the men, mostly skilled woodworkers (wood is a congenial material to the Russian) they were turning out skis and tennis racquets at a tremendous rate and seemed to be enjoying it. One jolly young expert, obviously not mentally defective or congenitally criminal in any way, told me that he was able to send his old father a substantial allowance out of the pocket money he earned at his ski making. I forebore to ask what he had done to bring him there; but there was certainly not a trace about him, or any of the men working with him, of the criminal type which our prisons produce. If they were ever like the young slouchers of that day's catch who had

frowned so at first, they had certainly been miraculously reformed. And there is nothing in the Russian system, as there
is in ours, to prevent all the other "prisons" being carried on
in the same way except those for the untameable human
wild beasts who are, I hope, sensibly and humanely liquidated, as they should be everywhere.

Thus the famous wild children of Russia, of whom the
Whites, and even some sentimental and now reactionary
Reds, have made so much political capital, are now captured, or grown up and assimilated, some of them very successfully, into the general body of citizens and even into the
Communist Party. Our forsytes made their plight much
worse by [their] backing up of all the counter-revolutionary
adventurers who undertook to restore the pleasant Bencken-
dorf dinners in London, and incidentally, of course, the
Tsardom. Still, it was only an episode, in which the Soviet
undertook the necessary social work which our forsytic Soviet at Westminster left to Dr Barnardo [39] and such money
as he could obtain by wasting half his priceless time in
begging. For please do not forget that a boy banditti has
long been a feature of British civilization, without the excuse of military devastation.

I pass on to the permanent and much more important
question of the education of the normal child who may possibly be a ruler and will certainly be a voter. What are the
inculcations which will form the second nature of the adult
if they are impressed early enough on the child?

With us the answer is easy. The inculcations are all
forsytic. I know this, because all the inculcations impressed
on me were forsytic; and if my pastors and masters had
been caught trying to make a Communist of me they would
have lost their jobs, and perhaps been prosecuted for blasphemy and sedition. When, in reaction against these incul-

cations,* and after my discovery of that side of history and my observation of that side of life which had been forsytically hidden from me or misrepresented to me, I perceived that civilization could be saved only by the extermination of the forsyte as a predatory and noxious species, I found that, far from my being in a position to exterminate them, the forsytes, thanks to this general forsytic inculcation, were in a position to exterminate me, and would certainly do it if they could comprehend my aims, which, fortunately for me, this topsy turvy education of theirs prevented them from doing. A project for their extinction was an enormity beyond the reach of their imagination. And so, at the age of 76, after a lifetime spent in dropping paper bombs charged with the most subversive explosives into their political, religious, and moral strongholds, I am still alive and at large, and even in some vogue among them as an amusing paradoxer.

How is it then that the leaders of the Russian revolution have been able to do what I cannot do: that is, set up an effective inquisition to enforce to the death the dogma that forsytism—parasitism—is the sin against the Holy Ghost, and that though all other sins may be forgiven, to it there is only one reaction: Bang!?

The answer is that before the outbreak of the suicidal European war which enabled those leaders to seize political power in Russia, they had received what I will call their tertiary education. Their elementary education was forsytic. Their secondary education was forsytic. Both were carefully planted on their minds in the Forsyte interest. That was my case too. But they picked up a third education for themselves just as I did. And in doing so they learned two things that changed their attitude towards Forsytism. These

* MS. has: inclucations

two things were, compendiously but precisely, as follows.

1. In the middle of [the] last century an educated professional class Jew named Karl Marx, of great mental and extraordinary literary power, to say nothing of German industry, devoted his life as an exile in London to the compilation of a voluminous essay on Capital, the effective god of the Forsytes, in which he brought an irresistible mass of official evidence to prove that the god, far from being the beneficent deity he seemed to the Forsytes, was the most abominable, cruel, and insatiable idol that had ever been set up even by his chosen race. Marx's thesis was that Capital, in unrestrained pursuit of profit in private hands, is capable of any atrocity, and, if not brought under public control and entirely cut off from the pursuit of private profit, must wreck civilization after centuries of the most frightful crimes against humanity. This literally epoch making essay changed the minds of the tertiarily educated throughout Europe.

2. The enormous extension of our historical knowledge which followed the death of Karl Marx revealed the fact that besides the Roman Empire with its old familiar decline and fall into the Dark Ages, there had existed at least half a dozen great civilizations which, after a development virtually just like that of our own civilization, had collapsed and perished from internal strain and corruption after exhibiting symptoms alarmingly like those of which all our advanced capitalistic States are at present complaining. This was rubbed in, not by a poor suburban revolutionist like Karl Marx, but by Sir Flinders Petrie, an archaeologist of unquestioned academic eminence, barnacled with official honors. It was in his respectable hands that the mighty empires of the past dwindled into bygone bankruptcies. When he saw three modern empires crash in the war of

1914–18 no poet sang "Stop; for thy tread is on an Empire's dust".[40] It was just as if three more brokers had been hammered on the Stock Exchange.

Now this was all booklearning. Books do not make revolutions at first hand. The effect of what we call an epoch making book is to direct dynamic attention to the author's view of real events and his explanation of them, if he has one. Such a book may be furiously denounced or derisively slighted on its first appearance; but if its readers find that current events are bearing it out, and that facts in the daily newspaper which meant nothing to them before become significant and memorable in the light of the book; if the misfortunes and miseries of their own to which they have submitted as Acts of God now reveal themselves as remediable faults in social construction; if they find themselves more and more driven first to the suspicion and then to the conclusion that the author was right after all on this point or that where he seemed to be ridiculously wrong, then the book will change the dynamic men's minds and make a new epoch. No book that is received at once with general applause is worth reading except as a work of art. It is the book that is burnt by the common hangman that makes history. It has been said of me by the superficial that I hate to be agreed with out of mere perversity. There is no perversity in the matter: I know that if I write a book that everyone agrees with I am wasting my time bringing coals to Newcastle.

Now what were the events that came under the observation of the tertiarily educated after their indoctrination by Marx?

First, capital went in pursuit of profit in Africa on the Congo and in South America on the Putumayo with a cruelty so filthy in its details and so ruthless in its greedy scoundrelism that the worst that has ever been judicially said of Nero or Torquemada would flatter it. And the particular Superforsyte who set the example was a near relative of Queen Victoria and a patron of all the Forsyte virtues. The reports of the factory inspectors quoted by Karl Marx are sickening enough; but they are Sunday reading compared to what Morel and Casement [41] revealed about the rubber boom. The forsytes denied and defended and lied and persecuted in their determination to hold on to their horrible profits; and they had the satisfaction later on of imprisoning Morel and hanging Casement on other scores; but Marx was justified nevertheless; and it presently appeared that all the vileness of which he convicted the pursuit of profit in our cotton factories are still in full swing under forsyte flags (including the Union Jack) in India and Japan and wherever capital is still free to do its worst in pursuit of private profit.

The only economic remedy which would bear scientific examination was Socialism, which involved a complete *volte-face* from Manchester Capitalism.[42] Unfortunately, this change of policy was supposed to be practicable through British parliamentary institutions; for it is the proudest pretension of those institutions that they provide a perfect political machinery for every possible change desired by the people under the most sacred "constitutional safeguards" of liberty. The millennium awaited only the achievement of Adult Suffrage. Whilst the franchise was still oligarchical, the Radical and Republican Left might still hold to the Liberal tradition that the masses must win their votes on the barricades, musket in hand; but when the Reform Acts of the nineteenth century, and their climax in the enfranchisement of women after the war, made the franchise as democratic as Votes for Everybody could make it, the last obstacle to the establishment of Socialism by parliamentary methods on the lines laid down by the Fabian Society seemed to have vanished.

Events soon exploded this delusion. The constitutional safeguards turned out to be safeguards not only against tyranny, but against any sort of governmental activity whatsoever beyond policing the field for Capitalism. Parliament was a wonderfully effective slow motion device for taking thirty years to do thirty minutes work, with, as I pointed out, the prospect of having some day to do thirty years work in thirty minutes or perish. Votes for Everybody, *alias* Democracy, was an ultra-Conservative force which could be stampeded into the maddest reaction at election time by any adroit stage manager with the Press at his command. A Labor Party in office in the House of Commons [43] dropped the subject of Socialism completely, reviled the Russian Communists, devoted the oratorical accomplishments it had learnt at the street corner and at the proletarian congresses to the unctuous utterances of the stalest Imperialist twaddle at Guildhall banquets, and finally disappeared in a crushing and richly deserved defeat at the polls, its leaders having saved their skins by accepting the high command on the Conservative side just before the discovery that the Conservatives could have done quite as well without them.

But this was not all. Something much more serious had happened long before the Labor *débacle*. The passage of an Act granting Home Rule to Ireland after the usual thirty years of parliamentary obstruction had been checkmated by armed forsyte rebellion and military mutiny in the commissioned ranks of the army. The Liberal Prime Minister had publicly assured the rebels that they would not be coerced, and had connived at their importations of arms

whilst vigorously coercing the Nationalists who were help-
ing themselves similarly. In the end the matter was decided, not by parliamentary action and acceptance of the
verdict of a majority of representatives, but by slaughter in
the field, assassination in the streets, and competitive house
burning in the counties. Ireland, fighting under a military
dictatorship called Sinn Fein, won, and, having thus demonstrated the futility and inefficiency of parliamentary
methods, was ironically rewarded with a parliament of its
own, which, after a brief but ferocious civil war, established
its authority by substituting bureaucratic triumvirates for
the local democratic governing bodies, by ruthless Coercion
Acts [44] rubbed in by hard flogging in the manner of Nicholas II and Stolypin,[45] and finally by an unprecedented
extension of martial law which gave five military commissioners power to execute anyone they pleased in Ireland,
with the result that though all the Opposition gunmen
promptly fled the country, the next general election brought
them all back again by placing their party in power in a
transport of reaction.

Meanwhile a few years of war waged by compulsory
military service and the conversion of party government
into military dictatorship by coalition and Defence of the
Realm Acts (martial law, in fact),[46] had removed from the
European system three decaying and poisonous empires
which would have survived centuries of parliamentary sham
warfare, but had replaced them with nothing better than
a chaos of republics and "constitutional monarchies" (meaning monarchies with the monarch bound hand and foot and
gagged) in which parliaments footled and squabbled helplessly whilst adventurers who were able enough or auda-
cious enough (or both) to make themselves dictators did
here and there contrive to do some cleaning up in the teeth

of parliamentary Liberalism, which shrieked far more loudly than Freedom did when Kosciusko fell.

Even militarism could not be trusted when it was "constitutional". The Dreyfus case, in which the officers of the French Army connived at an impudent forgery to drive out of their messrooms into the most horrible extremity of penal servitude an innocent Jew who after his rehabilitation served with distinction in the big war, destroyed the tradition of "the honor of the army", and made an end of the romantic presumption that an officer is necessarily a gentleman.

Our great stabilizing traditions could not stand up against such a series of shocks. Faith in them curdled into cynicism. Perhaps the most powerful of the old gods was Public Opinion. Nineteenth century statesmen like Gladstone had a real respect for this beneficent and upright force of the social conscientiousness, political intelligence, and fundamental rightmindedness of the English people. Consequently, as long as the restriction of the franchise left these virtues of Public Opinion entirely to the imagination of historians and statesmen, it was an effective force: Governments were really restrained from tyranny by their belief that Public Opinion would not allow it. The extension of the franchise, by enabling Public Opinion to express itself as what it really was, demolished this castle-in-the-air. Even when it understood what the Government was doing, which hardly ever happened, it could not remember it for a week. The twentieth century statesmen abandoned all pretence of respect for Public Opinion. From Asquith registering the population and assuring the public solemnly that this had no reference to compulsory military service and that no such unheard-of infraction of Liberty was in contemplation, and then introducing compulsory military service on that

registration, to Mr Ramsay Macdonald calling on the nation to save the gold standard and with it the very existence
of civilization by heroic sacrifices of their salaries and their
unemployment benefit, and, when the sacrifices were made,
immediately announcing that the only step which could
save the country from ruin was the abandonment of the
gold standard,[47] we have had proof after proof of the fact
that a British statesman can use all his eloquence to deny,
disclaim, and denounce on Tuesday the measure he fore-
sees he shall be obliged to take on Friday, when his eloquence will be turned on again to represent it as the
splendid gesture to which all patriotic citizens must rally.
This is called reassuring Public Opinion. It is the doll the
dentist gives a child to play with before he extracts its
teeth.

After all this, it is impossible to take our constitutional
catchwords seriously. To imagine they will stop Communism is silly. Liberty, the most hackneyed of all the catchwords, lost its last scrap of authority when compulsory
military service sent us all, rich and poor alike, like sheep
to the trenches. Does anyone suppose it will prevent us from
being sent to the benches when Communism demands compulsory industrial, agricultural, and business service for all,
rich and poor alike? No: the catchword bulwarks of the
old order are down: the forsytes have nothing to say for
themselves on constitutional lines. The Irish business has
demonstrated that though forsytes tolerate parliaments and
representative government as long as they are represented
by a ten to one majority, and have the Cabinet half in their
hands and wholly under their thumbs, and though they
even submit to ransom their riches and bribe the proletariat
to keep quiet up to a bearable point of taxation, yet the
moment their Forsytism is seriously challenged they cry

"To your tents, O Israel!" [48] Property will borrow from
Ulster the cry "The owners will fight; and the owners will
be right." The parasitic proletariat, from the Bond St shop-
keepers to the gamekeepers['] cottages, will rally to them.
Mercenary adventurers will not fail them whilst they can
pay; and all the forces of blind Conservatism and "Funda-
mentalism" will be on their side. Whether on such provoca-
tion the productive proletariat will marshal the unemployed
and go forth to war, and if so when and how, remains to
be seen. They have too often let themselves be bullied,
bludgeoned, and humbugged to raise any confident presumption that they will not do so again if property will only
make their condition bearable. But can it, even if it will?
Marx said no; and just at present it looks as if Marx was
right.

Thus every big incident of the century confirms the tertiarily educated in their Marxian view of capitalistic civilization. The bourgeoisie is rotten. The army is rotten. The
monarchies are rotten. Above all, parliamentary institutions
are rotten. And what has rotted them all to the core is
Capital in private hands in pursuit of private profit.

And now what was the effect on the secondarily educated,
the heads packed with forsytism at the secondary schools
and universities who regarded themselves as finished prod-
ucts, and never dreamt of such a possibility as tertiary
education?

If a university were anything like what it professes to be
it would have a special Faculty to hunt up all the heterodox
and controversial works of the moment and see that its students got the gist of them, and heard all there was to be
said for and against them. But the universities do the very
opposite. They avoid heterodox books as if they were
cobras; and the orthodoxy of their text books is not even

the orthodoxy of the day: it [is] an orthodoxy that dates from the Norman Conquest. They turn out a man with a first rate brain like Dean Inge, or a very lucid one like the late Earl of Oxford (Asquith), with a sociological equipment that is not merely obsolete but dangerously putrid; and when such a big opportunity for them as a book like Marx's Capital arrives, they do what they can to keep their students ignorant of its existence. When it breaks through by its own weight, they seize on the inevitable slips and errors which all human books contain (to say nothing of those rated as divine) and piffle about them as if the whole message and warning of the new prophet stood or fell by them. It is easy to pick holes in Marx. Like his great German rival Lassalle he had a streak of academic vanity, and was determined to shew that Socialism had come "equipped with all the culture of the age", and that the Socialists could beat the academic economists at their own game. He attached great importance to an analysis of the circulation of commodities which made his opening chapters very hard reading, and was a waste of his own time and the reader's, as the analysis was useless and the theory wrong. Half his pages, like those of Buckle,[49] consisted of references to books and pamphlets which lent no strength whatever to his case, and most of which I suspect he read no further than the first effective quotation. Such was the pretentious fashion of the day. He also occasionally parodied himself as a mathematician by stating his propositions in the form of very primitive equations, which was unfortunate at a moment when a school of genuine economist mathematicians, represented in England by Stanley Jevons, was arising to knock his pet theory of value into a cocked hat.[50]

With all this in hand the belittling of Marx was a cheap

job for any pedant; and I grieve to notice that some of the
ablest of my friends who have had the misfortune to qualify
themselves for university degrees, have acquired anti-Marx
reflexes which are ludicrously out of scale with the real
magnitude of the man. They seem to think that because
Marx was wrong and Jevons right as to the foundation of
value-in-exchange Jevons was an important economist and
Marx a negligible one. They forget that Jevons by his theory
of value confuted not only Marx but Adam Smith and
Ricardo. They forget that Jevons's contribution to the controversies roused by the immense development of state and
municipal enterprise to which Marx gave so momentous a
significance was a demonstration that a parcel post was
quite beyond the limits of Government enterprise: a thing
too silly to be remembered. When Marx shewed what the
pursuit of "surplus value" meant for civilization, and when
Ruskin revealed the abyss to which we were being led by
placing commercial values first and the moral values that
are beyond price nowhere,[51] what reply was it to them to
retort that neither of them understood the phenomenon of
rent of land or of General Walker's rent of ability?[52] The
socially important matter was that "surplus value" and its
pursuit by the ruthless plunder of nine tenths of the community by the remaining tenth are the basic facts of our
civilization, and that civilizations built on sand and sewage
cannot endure. These two great men, the Communist German Jew and the Tory British gentleman of independent
means, both shouted at the top of their voices that Europe
was on the quicksands. And Oxford and Cambridge responded with demonstrations that the seditious foreigner
and English fine art crank (the latter a dear good fellow,
bless his crazy soul, with a magnificent literary style) were

quite overlooking the extreme barreness [*sic*] of exces-
sively dry and hard soils, and were ignorant of the physical
constitution of both water and minutely divided silicates.

Marx rubbed into his readers the hopeless economic situation of the proletariat, because he held that when the proletarians became "class conscious" they would smash the
capitalist system. He might have gone on to say that if any
class, with the doubtful exception of the proprietary class,
understood its position, it would smash the capitalist system. The average professional or business competitor for a
livelihood has plenty of reasons for preferring Socialism to
Capitalism when he (or she) too, understands the position;
for they are all proletarians; and it is they, I should say,
who need economic and political self-consciousness much
more than the manual laborers. Marx, a bourgeois in violent
reaction against his own class, refuses to be troubled and
interrupted by the consideration that the proletariat is
partly bourgeois in fact and predominantly bourgeois in
aspiration. Though he was himself an example of the fact
that professional workers suffer more from poverty than
many skilled manual laborers, he had no time to bother
about trifles like that, and treated society in the large of
consisting of two classes, bourgeois and proletariat, plun-
derers and plundered. A perusal of Capital suggests that
Marx is not painting either the laborer or the employer
from the live model: his friend and collaborator Engels,
who was an employer, has a very different and more natural touch. In fact, Marx spent his life in a little clique of
ostracized Socialist refugees and their converts, all quite exceptional persons, either too good or too bad for the capitalist routine. He was a revolutionary recluse: his extraordinary power of invective against the bourgeoisie and his

faith in the capacity of the proletariat were never tempered
or weakened by actual intercourse with average specimens
of these animals.

H. G. Wells makes fun of Marx, but takes up his work of
creating "class consciousness" by going back to a classification of great simplicity and effectiveness.[53] He neither over-
rates the proletariat nor underrates the bourgeoisie. He says
that beneath all our modern social promiscuity, with its
suggestion that there is now no class distinction except between the propertied and the unpropertied (practically between grades of income) we still have three quite distinct
classes with distinct mentalities: a peasant class, a priestly
class, and a military class, though there is much masquerad-
ing of each in the other's clothes. Thus the peasant class
includes many big business bosses who know much about
contango [54] and nothing about turnips. The priestly class is
anti-clerical and anti-supernatural almost to a man (and
woman). The military class has its visible boundaries much
blurred, as its temperament no longer gravitates towards
the regular army and turns up in all the professions and
occupations or no occupations. Thus the names are only
historically significant and appropriate; for the modern
peasant is no longer a peasant; the modern priest is no
longer a priest nor his "clergy" any longer distinctive now
that everyone can read or write—or at least work a type-
writer; and the modern robber warrior no longer a soldier,
but a gangster. But the peasant mentality, the priest mentality, the robber and fighter mentality are all still distinct
and still functioning according to their nature. And they all
have to struggle with the revolutionist mentality, which
has emerged very distinctly in our time as the Marxist mentality.

The classical economists lumped all men into one class
or rather one species. According to them Man was an

animal who would do anything he was paid to do and nothing that he was not paid to do. And he would always prefer the work he was paid most for. He was An Economic Man. He is still a much ridiculed figment; but those who deride him should remember that though many people have natural vocations, so that a born clergyman will not be a stockbroker nor a born stockbroker a clergyman on any terms, yet, other things being equal, a stockbroker will prefer a fifty per cent commission to a five per cent one; and a clergyman will prefer a living worth five hundred a year to one worth one hundred and fifty. The economic man requires a much subtler study than the classic economists gave him, just as the bourgeois requires a subtler study than Marx gave him.

Let us accept Mr Wells's peasants, priests, and soldiers, as getters, thinkers, and predatory fighters. The secondarily educated will object that our actual class stratification does not correspond to it. But the secondarily educated may be swept out of the discussion by the well established reflex which responds to all their criticisms with the impatient exorcism "For God's sake, shut up". No scientific classification of political, social, or religious mankind can correspond to the facts as long as our family system imposes the father's habits of readymade thought on the son. The classification of men into Conservatives and Progressives, Ritualists [55] and Quakers, is none the less sound because there are plenty of pigheaded Conservatives in the Liberal Party and of fantastic Utopians among the Conservatives, or because half the members of a quaker [sic] family may be by temperament Anglo-Catholics * and a Neo-Platonist inheritor of the mantle of George Fox [56] may be Dean of St Paul's.[57] A scientific classification is not a list of traumatic dislocations, but of things according to their nature. When Mr

* MS. has: Angle-Catholics

Wells tells us that there are priests, soldiers, and peasants, and that the priest is distinguished by having neither ambition nor acquisitiveness [58] we must not interrupt him by shouts of "How about Wolsey? How about Alexander Borgia? How about old Snooks, the Bishop of Boodleby?" This or that cardinal may have been worldly, this or that soldier a coward: if so, it is they that have mistaken their professions, not Mr Wells who has mistaken the nature of their professions.

In Russia the triumphant Communists very soon found out that Mr Wells is right. In their constructive work they had to deal, not with two sorts of persons: bourgeois and proletarian, but with three sorts: persons who could and would work when somebody told them what to do after providing them with the necessary materials and instruments, and generally speaking making up their minds for them; peremptory people who could convey these instructions and see that they were obeyed; and people who could neither work nor bully, but whose natural vocation it was to think out what work should be assigned, what materials provided, what rules of conduct imposed, what religion inculcated upon children: roughly speaking the higher brain work, as we used to call it before we discovered that muscles as well as skulls have brains in them, and that some people can think much better with their fingers than with their heads.

The problem was to select these three sorts of people and, as the old rhyme goes, "to keep them in their proper stations" the associated prayer "God bless the squire and his relations" being dropped, partly because the Soviet did not believe in God, and partly because the squire and his relations had left hastily for Paris and considered himself only too happy to get there alive. If he could not do that he lay doggo, and said that his father was a peasant who worked with his hands on the land. The selection was difficult. Years ago I pointed out that what democracy lacked was a trustworthy anthropometric method.[59]

But the real classes, released from the traumatic pressure of private property and its consequences and reactions, soon asserted themselves as natural phenomena. Take a well-known instance. Djerjinsky,[60] who now reposes in his honored tomb in the Red Square in Moscow near Lenin, was given the urgent job of making the railways work. In the course of his efforts he sent a telegram to the staff of a certain railway station with certain instructions. Nothing happened. He sent a second telegram. Nothing happened. He sent a third. Nothing happened. Then something did happen. Djerjinsky put a revolver in his pocket and travelled to the irresponsive station. He assembled the staff and asked where his telegrams were. Nobody knew; but they were at last found in the waste paper basket in no danger of being attended to; for the station master and his assistants were dear lazy easygoing Russians who held the view which prevailed in the British Isles up to fifty years ago that a Government job is a sinecure. Djerjinsky thereupon produced the revolver, shot the two *fainéants,* and asked the rest whether they now realized that instructions were to be carried out and that a State railway station is not a casual ward for the ablebodied. The sincerity with which they admitted a strong impression to that effect was convincing; and from that station at least Djerjinsky had no further trouble. Thus did he pick himself out as an executive officer by his readiness to pick other people off if they stood in the way of the transport which was the circulation of Russia's life blood. And in some such fashion did the revolution discover and select all her managing directors. For the managing man, like the managing woman, soon asserts himself, not only through mere bumptiousness and coerciveness, but because the demand for him arises so instantly. His assumption of authority is not resented if he has reasonably good manners and the right sort of tact; for the cry of the workers is ever "Tell us what to do, governor" when there is the slightest hitch in their routine.

But how were the thinkers, Mr Wells's priest class, selected; and how were they kept sufficiently in touch with Demos to keep them aware of the effect of their experiments on his welfare and happiness and prevent them from going too fast for him or aiming too high over his head?

[Typed note in Ms.: New page here]

Here all old Liberal political students will exclaim against the dangers of indirect election. But what do they come to when weighed against the dangers, to say nothing of the impossibilities, of direct election[?] The objection to indirect election is that it weakens popular control. But when we come to the selections for which popular control is obviously not qualified, its removal to a point at which it is practically nullified is a gain, not a loss. As long as the alternative to popular control is nobbling by capitalist interests popular control may seem the lesser of two evils; but the contrast is delusive; for capitalist interests find it quite easy to nobble popular control: is not Tammany more securely rooted in popular control in New York than the old Metropolitan Board of Works was in indirect election in London? Who dares propose that the Cabinet should be directly elected by the populace, or the judicial committee of the Privy Council, or the Civil Service departments, or the Admiralty, or the War Office? The workman under Capitalism, as we know him, the trade unionist, is jealously "democratic" because he knows that his labor is being managed with a view to getting as much out of him for as little as possible, and to break him into submission to spoliation. But the Russian experiment shews that once a workman is convinced that he is being managed in his own interest, the difficulty is to induce him to attend the committees that are thrust on him by the managers who want to maintain contact with him so that whenever the shoe pinches they may hear of it at once. Thus Socialism, having destroyed Capitalist *Laissez-faire* in Russia, finds it rising again as the cry of the worker who doesn't want to be bothered with "workers' control", because it is extremely unpleasant to be burdened with a function for which one knows oneself to be unqualified, and if one is satisfied that the control is fair, and one is respected and sits in the best seats at the Opera and Ballet, and can always complain individually without being victimized, why should one be worried with brain work and talky-talky? One gets quite enough of that at the primary elections, where you can put a spoke in the wheel of any candidate who looks a wrong un, or who drinks, or who makes illicit love to respectable wives and daughters, who has played this or that shady trick and has nothing to bribe people with to vote for him? [*sic*]

Now comes the question, is there such a thing as a class which ought to be exterminated? Cromwell saw that the extermination of the Irish was a logical part of the policy of settling Ireland with English plantations. The extermination of the poor whites is a logical part of the existing policy of the Union of South Africa, though it is not explicitly set down in the programs of either the Nationalist or the South African Party. The red man has been exterminated in North America almost as extensively as the bison and more thoroughly than the rattlesnake. There is a demand everywhere outside Russia for the extermination of Communists, who, inside Russia, demand the extermination of capitalists. We appoint sheriffs to exterminate murderers; and Henry VIII did his best to exterminate tramps.[61] It is quite a mistake to suppose that there is anything distinctively Russian about weeding the garden. Recent efforts at reciprocal extermination [62] by the central empires plus Turkey and their neighbors plus the United States of America have been carried so far that it is still doubtful whether they have not succeeded in spite of the substitution for artillery in 1918 of the rancorous plundering ironically called the Peace. The prophecy put by Shakespear into the mouth of Antony has come to pass. "Blood and destruction shall be so in use that mothers shall but smile when they behold their infants quartered by the hands of war." [63] Millions of infants have within the recollection of people still quite young been not only quartered but smithereened by the hands of war; and everyday we dine with the quite ordinary and amiable young men who did it, and for doing it were called not merely trumps but aces. Let us therefore not in our discussions about Russia affect a squeamishness which we did not feel when we were put to the test ourselves. If we gloried in the slaughter of millions of young men "to make the world safe for democracy" we cannot afford to give ourselves moral airs when our most enterprising neighbor and former accomplice humanely and judiciously liquidates a handful of exploiters and speculators to make the world safe for honest men. The plain truth is that all civilized governments exact minimum standards of conduct which they enforce by killing the people who do not attain them. Our question is not to kill or not to kill, but how to select the right people to kill. The famous execution on Calvary, for instance, has never been challenged in respect of the two thieves who suffered on that occasion along with the Communist. The principle of the execution is fully admitted. All the controversies have arisen on the point whether the execution of the Communist was not a mistake—whether he was not rather the sort of person who should be encouraged rather than liquidated. Was he really an enemy of mankind or was he a saviour? Our general conclusion so far seems to be that, whether or no, we are well rid of him.

I think we go to the opposite extreme ourselves in glorifying thieves, provided their booty is big enough and they play the game according to the rules they have themselves made, meanwhile holding up that particular Communist as the prince of such thieves. But that is a matter of opinion. What I am now making clear is that Russia, in exterminating a particular sort of undesirable for the good of the rest is doing precisely what we are doing and always have been doing; and that the essential difference between the Russian liquidator with his pistol (or whatever his humane killer may be) and the British hangman is that they do not operate on the same sort of person.

Has Russia, then, in adding exploiters and parasites to the stock European list of the undesirable, taken a step in advance of Europe or merely made a mistake? However that question be answered no one who understands it can deny that she has a very strong case. The exploiter, as indicted by Karl Marx, has been proved deeply guilty; and the reasons for tolerating him, which were, first, that he was indispensable as there was no available alternative to his management and enterprise in industry; second, that he was making a glorious success of our affairs and establishing the reign of universal peace with its temple in the Crystal Palace [64] and its priests the Prince Consort and

Richard Cobden; and third, that his selfishness, if completely unrestrained, would spontaneously guarantee subsistence wages to a permanently employed proletariat whilst
at the same time providing an entirely leisured body of expensively cultivated persons [to] patronize art and science,
govern the country as an elegant recreation, officer the army,
maintain our command of the sea against all foreign poach-
ers on that important preserve of Britannia's, and act generally as the repository of culture, the glass of fashion and
the mould of form, besides—this above all—becoming so
enormously rich that he could not possibly spend all his
money, and, even after indulging in every practicable ex-
travagance of luxury, must automatically accumulate and
invest capital out of sheer inability to spend his income.
This latter item was rather like burning the house to roast
the pig: still, there was no apparent alternative a hundred
years ago.

None of these pleas will hold good today. It is true that
in Russia the peasant, the Kulak (bigger farmer), and the
private trader, each working for his own hand, are still
indispensable as auxiliaries * to Communism, and that a pre-
mature attempt to exterminate them produced such a serious shortage that they had to be reinstated provisionally to
some extent. But their indispensability is vanishing as large
scale communal farming, national industrialism, and cooperative distribution encroaches on them and sweeps their
business into the dustbin just as big capitals sweep petty
capitals in the west. The superfluous income of the rich on
which we used to depend for fresh capital, [is] † being
confiscated on such a scale that the necessity for allowing
it to pass through the capitalist's hands at all is a mockery
even to himself: an industrial government can find its own

---

* MS. has: auxilliaries   † MS. has: are

capital as easily as any big capitalistic trust can and does provide its own reserves. As to his millennial promises of universal peace and steady employment, war, on a scale that would have staggered Napoleon, has become chronic since the great exhibition; unemployment has never ceased for a single day and has now attained gigantic and still growing proportions; distribution, always grotesquely and mischievously anomalous, has been broken down by unregulated competitive production; and as to the moral and cultural pretensions, only a rigidly restrictive factory code has saved the proletariat from hideous degradation, misery, and finally destruction. Karl Marx and the Hammonds [65] may have made the story readable, as poet Crabbe and others had done before; but it is all in the official reports of the factory inspectors for those who mistrust the fierce humanitarian bias of its literary describers.

As against all this, what is to be said for the people who will not, if they can help it, allow any of us to eat, drink, sleep, work, lie in our graves, or even watch and pray unless they can make a profit out of our doing so in some form[?] Why may I not write plays in London without paying every year to some person who has the power to order me off the earth a sum that would keep five working class families[?] Why should I have to earn his living for him on pain of not being allowed to earn my own? The answer in my individual case is simple. I am a proprietor as well as a worker. I rob Peter to pay Paul. I allow Paul to rob me because he connives at my robbing Peter. We two are in the same swim. But the vast majority of workers have no such corrupt motive for harboring parasites and sustaining exploiters. They have to earn every farthing they are robbed of. Under our system they can extricate themselves from this position only by becoming robbers themselves; and though everything is done to persuade them that they have a fair chance of doing this if they are good boys and girls, their chance is really negligible unless, like me, they happen to possess a talent which is not only very exceptional but highly lucrative.

A century ago, when Socialism had not come into the field of possibilities, economists, jurists, and political philosophers were quite frank on these points. They painted the lot of the proletariat without any rose color because there was no visible or thinkable alternative. They approved quite honestly of the penalisation of all attempts at mitigation by trade unionism as mischievous interferences with freedom of contract and competition which must finally prove futile. In those days the name co-operator was a more infamous brand than Bolshy is now. But when co-operation, nationalization of land, trade unionism in its Owenite phase, Christian Socialism,[66] and finally the "Scientific Socialism" of Lassalle and Marx came into vogue as possible alternatives to Capitalism, the old frankness was dropped; and Capitalism was no longer presented as the reasoned scientific system it actually is, but as a masquerade of heroes of private enterprise getting rich quickly and scattering all the blessings of civilization on prospering populations which owed everything to them. Political economy was "banished to Saturn" and replaced by the glorified image of Cecil Rhodes. This transfiguration was easy at first, because until quite recent times the earth was so poorly and ignorantly cultivated that when the arts of production suddenly developed scientifically, and finance became so complicated that only a few people could handle it (mostly without understanding it), it became possible for exploiters first, and financiers later on, to become fabulously rich: so rich, in fact, that it cost men who began as mere acquisitive animals nothing to become living founders of good works, to feel no longer mean and dishonest, and to experience that delight in being a saint which only a born scoundrel can really relish. It was an expensive way of producing saints; but it was glamorous and therefore popular.

I do not believe that these saints of plutocracy (one of the first, by the way, was Robert Owen, the founder of English Utopian Socialism) had any fundamental understanding of the system by which they had become rich. When they attempted to work outside the system, or against it, as Owen did, they often made the most childish mistakes. From Owen trying to start his new moral world in the Grays Inn Road [67] to Mr Ford chartering a ship to stop the big war by a mission of naïve pacificists,[68] we have had instance after instance of the fact that the secret of these great money makers was that they were energetic and modest and single-minded enough always to try to make it on whatever scale was within their reach, and simple enough to believe that they would win through if they kept pegging away. When circumstances were propitious they succeeded: when the chase was a wild goose one, they failed. In neither case had they seen much further than the ends of their noses.

* *

ADDENDA

[Shaw's MS. concludes with a postcard containing holograph notes, in ink, for material intended for inclusion in a redrafting of the text. Shaw's page references in these notes refer to the pages of his original MS. The text of the notes is as follows:]

Russian MS.

p 5 [p. 43 of the present book] redraft. The ransom could have been paid, but not the ransom plus the interest on British investments.

p 12 [p. 50 of the present book] Add the assumption that a proletariat has no right to live unless it can render services worth its keep to the proprietariat.

Add also the notion that the export of capital enriches a country, and that an excess of exports over imports is a favorable balance of trade.

Notes

Preface

1. This criticism of Gladstone appeared in the first edition (1920) of Wells's *Outline of History,* but was eliminated from subsequent editions.

2. R. H. Tawney (1880–1962), English socialist and political philosopher, author of *The Acquisitive Society,* London, 1926.

3. Henry Mayers Hyndman (1842–1921), English socialist and writer. From 1881 he was an active Marxist. He founded the Social Democratic Federation, which was replaced in 1911 by the British Socialist Party. Hyndman withdrew from the party in 1916 as a gesture of opposition to its policies.

Karl Johann Kautsky (1854–1938), German socialist leader and anti-Bolshevik Marxist.

Pavel Nikolaevich Miliukoff (1859–1943), founder of the Russian Constitutional Democratic Party. In 1905 he brought together all the liberal groups in the Duma in an organization called the Union of Unions, whose aim was to achieve universal suffrage and a true parliamentary government for Russia. During 1917 Miliukoff became Minister of Foreign Affairs in Prince Lvov's provisional government, but he fled into exile after the October Revolution.

Alexander Kerensky (1881–   ), Russian social democrat who played a leading role in the revolution of February 1917. He became premier in July of that year, but was deposed by the Bolsheviks in the October Revolution.

4. The "academic ghoul" was Sir William Matthew Flinders Petrie (1853–1942), English Egyptologist, who also made notable excavations at Stonehenge and in Palestine. Shaw makes similar allusions to Flinders Petrie in the preface to *Back to Methuselah*.

5. The phrase following the comma is taken from Prospero's famous speech in *The Tempest,* IV.i.154–156.

6. The simile, alluding to *The Rhine Gold,* is natural to Shaw the Wagnerian and author of *The Perfect Wagnerite.* "Fafnir goes off with his booty . . . Merely to prevent others from getting it is the only purpose it brings him. He piles it in a cave, transforms himself into a dragon . . . and devotes his life to guarding it. . . ." *Major Critical Essays,* Standard Edition, p. 183.

7. Buxton in Derbyshire, England is noted for its severe winter weather. During and after heavy snowfalls the schoolboys of Buxton College, some forty or fifty years ago, used tea trays for sliding on the ice. The custom is no longer practiced.

8. The Glorious Revolution of 1688 which deposed James II in favor of William III and Mary. William III was succeeded by Anne, Mary's sister. Anne died without leaving any children, and by the terms of the Act of Settlement (1701), George I, son of Sophia of Hanover, who had been designated Anne's heir but had predeceased her, became the first Hanoverian king of England.

9. Menenius Agrippa, who tells his fable in Shakespeare's *Coriolanus,* I.i.94–160.

10. The linen-draper, John Gilpin, whose unfortunate adventures in trying to ride a horse are recounted in the famous poem by William Cowper (1731–1800). The location of Gilpin's shop in London is given in the eleventh verse.

Chapter One

1. Marie Thérèse Louise de Savoie-Carignan, Princess de Lamballe (1749–1792), superintendent of Marie Antoinette's household. She returned from exile in England to share her queen's fate. The Princess refused to take the oath of detestation

of the French monarchy, and was massacred as she stepped out of the court room.

2. The allusion is to Mme. Defarge in Dickens's *Tale of Two Cities* (1859); similar scenes occur in the "Scarlet Pimpernel" novels of Baroness Orczy.

3. "In 1894, Henry Hutchinson, who had provided the funds for much of our [Fabian Society] country lecturing, died, and to our complete surprise it was found that he had appointed Sidney Webb . . . his executor, and had left the residue of his estate, between £9000 and £10,000, to five trustees . . . with directions that the whole sum be expended within ten years. . . . The trustees . . . decided to devote part of the funds to initiating the London School of Economics and Political Science because they considered that a thorough knowledge of these sciences was a necessity for people concerned in social reconstruction. . . ." E. R. Pease, *The History of the Fabian Society*, London, 1916, pp. 123–124. The London School of Economics was admitted as part of the University of London in 1900.

4. Ferdinand Johann Gottlieb Lassalle (1825–1864), German social democrat, writer and revolutionary; he was active in the revolution of 1848.

5. Prince Peter Kropotkin (1842–1921), the "anarchist Prince," mathematician, geographer, philosopher, and Nihilist-revolutionary.

6. English Fabians: members of a socialist society founded in London on January 4, 1884. The society, which is still active, took its name from Quintus Fabius Maximus Cunctator ("the Delayer"), a Roman general who achieved victory by a strategy of skilfully avoiding direct conflict. The Fabians studied Marx intensively, but put their faith in Jevons and J. S. Mill, and in the evolution of socialism through a policy of political permeation of existing institutions rather than through revolution. Sidney Webb described the society's policy as the inevitability of gradualness. The society is affiliated to the Labor Party and has exerted considerable influence on it. Shaw first attended a Fabian meeting on May 16, 1884, and was elected a member of the society on September 5 of the same year. Subsequently he wrote many of the Fabian tracts and edited *Fabian Essays in Socialism*, 1889.

7. White Fathers are members of the Society of African Missionaries, founded in 1868 by the Abbé Lavigerie. They dress in white and are active in northern and equatorial Africa.

8. Karl Freiherr vom Stein (1757–1831), a Prussian Liberal statesman whose reforms laid the foundations of his country's greatness. He abolished hereditary serfdom, reorganized municipal government, eliminated monopolies, reformed the tax and financial system, and reconstituted the army on a basis of universal conscription. After 1810 Stein's reforms were completed by the chancellor, Karl August Fürst von Hardenberg (1750–1822), who also reorganized the Prussian educational system.

9. The triumph of Free Trade in England occurred during the period between 1820 and 1850, following the retraction by Parliament of duties between England and Ireland. This retraction was the outcome of protests by the Manchester Chamber of Commerce. Subsequently, the Manchester School became preoccupied with Anti-Corn Law League propaganda. See also note 42.

10. Shaw is referring to the triumph of the Meiji interests in 1867–1868. Mutshuhito, the new Japanese emperor, brought to an end the long dominance of feudal military government, and agreed to establish a parliamentary system. His supporters organized a centralized bureaucratic administration and abandoned anti-foreign imperial policies. Japan thereupon embarked on a great period of modernization.

11. Anne Robert Jacques Turgot (1727–1781), French economist who successfully pursued a free trade policy in France until he was dismissed from office by Louis XVI. Turgot's major work, *Réflexions sur la formation et la distribution des richesses* (1766), is the best expression of the economic theories of the Physiocrats. Richard Cobden (1804–1865) and John Bright (1811–1889) were leaders of the Manchester School of English free-traders. See further note 42.

12. Joseph Smith (1805–1844), founder of the Mormon religion. His *Book of the Mormon* (1830) was claimed to be the work of a prophet named Mormon.

13. Joanna Southcott (c. 1750–1814), an English fanatic who claimed to be the woman mentioned in *Revelations* xii. She

prophesied that she would be the mother of a new Messiah called Shiloh, and attracted a considerable body of followers.

14. Karl Marx and his family moved to a house at 9 Grafton Terrace, Maitland Park, Haverstock Hill, near Hampstead Heath, London, in the autumn of 1856. Marx lived here until his death in 1883.

15. Hyndman pointed this out in the fourteenth chapter of his *Evolution of Revolution,* London, 1920. That section of the book is devoted to the Peruvian economic and social system before the advent of the Spanish Conquistadores.

16. "In Russia I must confess my passive objection to Marx has changed to a very active hostility. Wherever we went we encountered busts, portraits, and statues of Marx. About two-thirds of the face of Marx is beard, a vast solemn woolly uneventful beard that must have made all normal exercise impossible. . . . It is exactly like *Das Kapital* in its inane abundance. . . . Some day, if I am spared, I will take up shears and a razor against *Das Kapital;* I will write *The Shaving of Karl Marx.*" Wells, *Russia in the Shadows,* New York, 1921, ch. III, "The Quintessence of Bolshevism."

17. This occurred in 1884. The Rev. Philip Wicksteed, a Jevonian (see note 50), maintained that he had discerned fallacies in Marx's theory of value. He was challenged by the Fabian Society to prepare a criticism of Marx, and this critique was published as "*Das Kapital:* A Criticism," in *Today* for October 1884. Shaw was invited to defend Marx against Wicksteed's argument, but on applying himself to the subject he came to the conclusion that Wicksteed was right. See further *Bernard Shaw and Karl Marx: A Symposium 1884–1889* (New York, 1930), in which the articles of Shaw and Wicksteed are reprinted.

18. In *The Koran,* sura XVI, Mahomet says that Allah had "thrown firm mountains on the earth, lest it move." Mahomet's calendar proved "disastrously wrong" when, in later centuries, caravans began to go astray in their seasonal crossing of the desert.

19. Pierre-Joseph Proudhon (1809–1865). His maxim, "La propriété c'est le vol," occurs in the first chapter of his *Qu'est-ce que la Propriété?* (1840). In "The Revolutionist's Handbook,"

Man and Superman, Standard Edition, p. 216, Shaw comments that Proudhon's proposition is "the only perfect truism that has been uttered on the subject" of property.

20. Marx's quarrel with Proudhon was sparked by the latter's abandonment of the struggle for revolution and of "dogmatism" in economic matters. Proudhon claimed that he had solved the property question in a new book, published in 1846, which he had subtitled "The Philosophy of Poverty." Marx accordingly entitled his vigorous response "The Poverty of Philosophy." The quarrel with Bakunin began when he challenged Marx's leadership at the International of 1869. But in the Hague Congress of 1872 Marx triumphed and Bakunin was outvoted and expelled from the International. Marx severed his association with Hyndman in 1881, when the latter published *England for All,* a presentation of the policy of the Social Democratic Federation. It appeared to Marx that Hyndman had plagiarized sections of *Das Kapital,* and Marx himself was nowhere mentioned by name in Hyndman's book.

21. The Tichborne Case involved the claim of an impostor, Arthur Orton (1834–1898), to the estate of the deceased Roger Charles Tichborne. On May 11, 1871, Orton brought an ejectment action against the trustees of the estate. During the long trial that ensued, the jury concluded that the claimant was an impostor, in consequence of the refusal of his counsel, Edward Kenealy, to put Orton's sisters in the box as witnesses. Orton was arrested, tried for perjury, found guilty on two counts, and sentenced to penal servitude for fourteen years.

22. *"Pons asinorum"* is a figurative expression signifying a difficulty that must be overcome if one is to proceed further with one's studies. A scholar stopped by the *pons asinorum* will never be capable of further progress in his chosen subject. Shaw explains the law of economic rent in "The Economic Basis of Socialism," the first of his *Essays in Fabian Socialism,* and includes knowledge of the "theory of rent" in his anthropometric test for the selection of rulers, outlined in the preface to *Farfetched Fables* (see further note 59).

23. Mariya Aleksandra Spiridonova assassinated General Luzhenovsky, brutal commandant of the district of Boris-Soglebsk, on January 16, 1906. Spiridonova was twenty-one years old. As

Luzhenovsky lay dying of his bullet wounds, his Cossacks, led by an officer called Avramov, set upon the assassin and beat her savagely with whips and knouts. At the police station Spiridonova was subjected to even more brutal assaults. See I. Steinberg, *Spiridonova*, London, 1935.

24. Evident in the many pamphlets of Tolstoy's later years as well as in such writings as *What Then Must We Do?* (1886), *The Kingdom of God Is within You* (1893), and *The Christian Doctrine* (1897).

25. The paraphrase "weeding the garden" is borrowed from Shaw's friend, Dean Inge (1860–1954), called the "Gloomy Dean" by reason of the overcast nature of his philosophy. The expression "weeding the garden" is amusingly attributed to the Chinese philosopher Dee Ning in the first act of part IV of *Back to Methuselah*.

26. James II replaced by William III. See further note 8.

27. Jean Paul Marat (1743–1793) was eminent as a medical practitioner and physiologist before he became involved in the politics of the French Revolution. As a doctor he witnessed the sufferings of his impoverished patients.

28. Georges Cadoudal (1771–1804), a royalist conspirator and leader of the Chouan partisans during the French Revolution. Cadoudal was guillotined for being implicated with Charles Pichegru in a conspiracy against Napoleon Bonaparte. There is no evidence that the Chouan leader was ever a socialist.

29. Sir Francis Galton (1822–1911), a cousin of Charles Darwin, developed new methods in statistics. His greatest achievement in this field was the correlational calculus.

30. Marshal Ney, for example, was a cooper's son; Marshal Masséna, perhaps Napoleon's greatest general, was originally a cabin boy. Emil Ludwig says that Napoleon's generals were men "drawn from the dregs of society out of whom their commander, the youngest of them all, was soon to make heroes and generalissimos, and subsequently princes and dukes."

31. Lev Davidovich Bronstein, alias Leon Trotsky (1879–1940), was the son of a wealthy peasant farmer. V. I. Lenin, born Vladimir Ilyitch Ulyanov (1870–1924), was the son of an inspector of schools at Simbirsk. Iosif Vissarionovich Dzhugashvili, later known as Stalin (1879–1953), was born in Transcau-

casian Georgia, and educated at Tiflis Theological Seminary. His
father, a shoemaker, died when the boy was eleven. Iosif was
brought up by his mother, a poor washerwoman who lavished all
that she could afford on her son.

32. For example, the Gordon Riots in London, June 1780.
They were the expression of mob protest at the repeal of certain
penal laws against the Roman Catholics.

33. An allusion to the suppression and dissolution of the mon-
asteries and the confiscation of their property during 1536–1539.
In *The Intelligent Woman's Guide* Shaw notes that "Henry VIII,
a royal Leader, plundered the Church and made it a crime to be
a Catholic priest; but he immediately had to disgorge his booty
and distribute it among his prefects and their families."

34. Samuel Smiles (1812–1904), Scottish social reformer; a
kind of Victorian Dale Carnegie. His famous book, *Self-Help*
(1857), presented model lives of great men and offered the advice, "Do thou likewise."

35. Correctly, "The red fool-fury of the Seine." Shaw is quot-
ing Tennyson, *In Memoriam*, cxxvii.

36. John Elliott Cairnes (1824–1875). In a discussion of production and consumption arising out of his consideration of the
meaning of value, Cairnes concludes, "I think it is important,
on moral no less than on economic grounds, to insist upon this,
that no public benefit of any kind arises from the existence of
an idle rich class. The wealth accumulated by their ancestors or
others on their behalf, where it is employed as capital, no doubt
helps to sustain industry; but what they consume in luxury and
idleness is not capital, and helps to sustain nothing but their
own unprofitable lives. By all means they must have their rents
and interest, as it is written in the bond; but let them take their
proper place as drones in the hive, gorging at a feast to which
they have contributed nothing." (*Some Leading Principles of
Political Economy*, 1878, p. 35.) As Shaw suggests, Cairnes rejected socialism. In an earlier book, *Essays in Political Economy*,
Cairnes observed that socialism is a "rank growth of economic
ignorance" and that it breeds despotism, "and despotism, when
it is finished, issues in war, misery, and ruin."

37. See Shaw's critical analysis of *The Valkyrie* in *Major Critical Essays*, Standard Edition, 192 ff. The theme of the highest

being setting to work at his own extinction and replacement by a new superbeing is, of course, a motif in *Man and Superman* as well as in Nietzsche.

38. Shaw's special interest in this problem was stimulated during his stay in the U.S.S.R. (see Introduction to this book) by his visit to a reformatory center for juvenile delinquents, and by his impressions of the Soviet film *Road to Life*, which dealt with the rehabilitation of Russia's homeless and orphaned children.

39. Thomas John Barnardo (1845–1905), British philanthropist, founder and director of homes for waifs and orphans.

40. The line occurs in Byron's *Childe Harold*, III.xvii.

41. E. D. Morel (1873–1924), journalist and humanitarian; Sir Roger David Casement (1864–1916), Irish patriot and one-time British consular official. While he was British consul at Boma, Casement investigated the Belgian rubber trade in the upper Congo. The Congo Free State was then ruled despotically by Leopold II of Belgium. Leopold's policy was ruthless exploitation of the vast rubber resources, and the victims of his exploitation were the African native workers, of whom between five and eight millions were worked to death or otherwise murdered in fulfilling rubber quotas. Casement's official report of 1903 exposed the "red rubber" atrocities. In England an anti-Congo campaign was directed by E. D. Morel, who became honorary secretary of the Congo Reform Association. The shocked reactions of international public opinion eventually compelled Leopold and the Belgian government to set up a Commission of Inquiry which led to drastic changes in the conditions and administration in the Congo. The subsequent fates of Morel and Casement were as Shaw has briefly indicated. Casement was executed by the British for high treason in consequence of his landing in Ireland by German submarine to foment a Sinn Fein revolt. (See Shaw's pamphlet, *A Discarded Defense of Roger Casement*, 1922.) Morel was arrested in August 1927 and charged under the Defense of the Realm Act with having "unlawfully and wilfully, without permit from the Admiralty or Army Council, convey[ed] and transmit[ed] from the United Kingdom to a neutral country (Switzerland) a pamphlet, contrary to the said regulations." Morel had, in fact, sent to a correspondent in Paris, Miss Ethel

Sidgwick, a copy of his pamphlet, *Tsardom's Part in the War,*
which was to be forwarded to the distinguished French writer,
Romain Rolland. Morel claimed that he did not know then that
Rolland was living in Switzerland (a neutral country). The magistrate refused to grant bail and Morel was confined in Brixton
prison. At his trial he again contended that he had not wilfully
broken the law, but despite a spirited defense, he was sentenced
to six months in Pentonville.

42. The Manchester School is the name applied to a group of
English free-trade capitalists active mainly between 1820 and
1850. Much of their work involved Anti-Corn Law League propaganda. Their leaders were John Bright and Richard Cobden,
whose *laissez-faire* doctrines were influenced by the economic
theories of David Ricardo (1772–1823) and Adam Smith (1723–
1790). See note 9.

43. These events occurred during J. Ramsay MacDonald's first
ministry (Jan.–Nov. 1924) and his second ministry (1929–
1931). MacDonald's third ministry was a National Coalition, not
a Labor Government.

44. The Sinn Feiners set up their own independent Irish parliament, the Dail Eireann, in 1919. Ten years later, in the face of
recurring dissent and insurrection by De Valera's new Republican Society, a splinter group that had arisen in denunciation of
Irish partition and the settlement with England, the Dail passed
a public safety act authorizing the establishment of military
tribunals to deal with illegal Republican Army activities.

45. Flogging was a common punishment for military indis-
cipline and civilian misdemeanors during the reign of Tsar
Nicholas II (1884–1917) and under the premiership of Pëtr
Arkadevich Stolypin (1863–1911).

46. Shaw was still infuriated with the British Defense of the
Realm Act (4 & 5 Geo 5., cc. 29, 63) introduced during the
First World War and effectively retained by the government
until August 31, 1921, the date fixed by Order in Council as the
termination of the war. Shaw's most vigorous criticism of the
D.O.R.A. is to be found in his journalism of the war years, subsequently collected and reprinted as *What I Really Wrote about
the War.*

47. The gold standard was abandoned by Britain on September 21, 1931.

48. This is familiar to Shavians and Fabians as the title of an attack by Shaw and Sidney Webb on the Liberal Government of the 1890s. It was later published in an expanded form as *A Plan of Campaign for Labour,* Fabian tract no. 49 (1894).

49. Henry Thomas Buckle (1821–1862), English historian, author of the unfinished *History of Civilization in England* (1857–1861). In the appendix to his *Intelligent Woman's Guide* Shaw observed that Buckle's *History* presents a conception of historical materialism comparable to Marx's but offering a different moral: "to wit, that progress depends on the critical people who do not believe everything they are told: that is, on scepticism."

50. William Stanley Jevons (1835–1882), English economist and logician, author of *The Theory of Political Economy,* 1871. Jevons was one of the first economists to advance the concept of final or marginal utility. He attacked the labor-cost theory of value and all other cost theories, and maintained that the value of any commodity fluctuates according to the extent of its utility.

51. John Ruskin (1819–1900). In 1860 Ruskin began to propound a new social system, denouncing the dogmas of political economy expounded by J. S. Mill and the Benthamites. In a series of lectures, Ruskin denied the productivity of exchange and attacked interest as distinct from usury. The papers on which these lectures were based were published as *Unto This Last.*

52. Francis Amasa Walker (1840–1897), American economist, apostle of free trade and bimetallism. He rose from private to brigadier general during the Civil War. Walker became Professor of Political Economy and History at Yale (1873–1881) and President of Massachusetts Institute of Technology (1881–1897). On his rent of ability see Walker's books, *Money in Its Relation to Trade and Industry* and *Land and Its Rent.*

53. The allusion is to *The Outline of History.* Wells actually lists twelve classes: (1) the priesthood, (2) the nobility, (3) the tillers of the soil, (4) the artisans, (5) the herdsmen, (6) the merchants, (7) the small retailers, (8) the independent property owners, (9) the domestic servants, (10) gang workers—slaves, prisoners of war, etc., (11) mercenary soldiers, (12) seamen.

Wells observes that "The civilization in which we live today is simply carrying on and still further developing and working out and rearranging these relationships. This is the world from which we inherit." (*The Outline of History*, Book III, ch. 17).

54. Contango is a London Stock Exchange term signifying the premium or interest paid by a buyer to the seller in order to be permitted to defer payment until a future settlement.

55. On Ritualists see the dialogue between Sempronius and Pamphilius in the first act of *The Apple Cart*.

56. George Fox (1624–1691), founder of the Society of Friends, the Quakers. Fox is a character in Shaw's play, "*In Good King Charles's Golden Days.*"

57. The neo-Platonist inheritor of Fox's mantle was Shaw's friend, William Ralph Inge, Dean of St. Paul's, London. See note 25.

58. See *The Outline of History*, Book III, ch. 16, "Gods and Stars, Priests and Kings."

59. In "The Revolutionist's Handbook" to *Man and Superman*, 1903, Shaw had written: "Government presents only one problem: the discovery of a trustworthy anthropometric method." Chapter xxxvi of *Everybody's Political What's What?* (1944) is entitled "Our Attempts at Anthropometry." As late as the preface to *Farfetched Fables* (1950) Shaw observed that "What we need desperately is an anthropometric sliderule by which we can classify and select our rulers."

60. Feliks Edmundovich Djerjinsky (1877–1926), Soviet politician; organizer and first head (1917–1921) of the Cheka, the Soviet secret police, later renamed the G.P.U. As transport commissar (1921) he reorganized and greatly improved the Russian railroad system. Shaw cherished a photograph of Djerjinsky which is still on display at Shaw's Corner, Ayot St. Lawrence. The incident of the transport commissar is retold in the prefaces to *On the Rocks* (1933) and *The Simpleton of the Unexpected Isles* (1934). In the latter preface the organizer of the Cheka is referred to as "gentle Djerjinsky."

61. The Tudor kings and queens regarded vagrancy as a political menace. By law, in 1530, vagrants could be whipped and sent home. A statute promulgated in 1547, the last year of Henry

VIII's reign, condemned vagrants to slavery for a year for a first offense, life imprisonment for a second offense, and a felon's death for a third offense.

62. Extermination is the subject of the preface to *On the Rocks*, written in the year following Shaw's visit to the U.S.S.R.

63. The quotation is from *Julius Caesar*, III.i.266–269, but Shaw has omitted one of Antony's lines:

> "Blood and destruction shall be so in use,
> And dreadful objects so familiar,
> That mothers shall but smile when they behold
> Their infants quarter'd with the hands of war."

64. Paxton's famous glass structure erected to house London's Great Exhibition of 1851.

65. John Lawrence le Breton Hammond (1872–1949) and his wife, Barbara—authors of major works on the Industrial Revolution, including *The Village Labourer, 1760–1832* (1911), *The Town Labourer, 1760–1832* (1917), *The Skilled Labourer, 1760–1832* (1919), *The Rise of Modern Industry* (1925), and *The Age of the Chartists* (1930).

66. Between 1830 and 1834 Robert Owen (1771–1858), Scots socialist and reformer, had been leader of an embryonic trade union movement whose objective was to found cooperative productive societies that would take over entire industries. In the mid-nineteenth century Charles Kingsley, F. D. Maurice, and other Christian Socialists opposed *laissez-faire* capitalism with a Christian appeal for political and economic action on behalf of all the population. They first attempted, without much success, to set up small working associations. Later they tried to foster copartnership and profit-sharing in capitalist industry, and also a consumers' cooperative movement. See *Encyclopedia Britannica* (1963), article on "Socialism."

67. In 1834 Owen founded a journal, *The New Moral World*, concerned with his plans for the great moral revolution that he envisaged in the near future. His vision was communicated to a society of his disciples in London who called themselves the Association of All Classes of All Nations. Later, a book by Owen, *The Book of the New Moral World*, became, as his biographer

G. D. H. Cole calls it, "the Bible of the Owenites." The meeting-place of the Owenites was located in Gray's Inn Road, Holborn, London.

68. Shaw is referring to Henry Ford's peace mission of 1915. Ford was reported to have promised to "get the boys out of the trenches" by Christmas. Despite his failure to win the approval of President Wilson, and in the face of widespread ridicule by the press, Ford financed the expedition of a number of pacifist American celebrities who proceeded to Europe on the ship *Oscar II*. When it arrived in Norway, a permanent delegation was set up which persisted, financed by Ford, until 1917 when the U.S.A. entered the war.